China Livestreaming E-commerce Industry Insights

Ruo Si

China Livestreaming E-commerce Industry Insights

Research Team: Meng Tang, Xinxin Song, Hang Li, Fayan Wang, Ying Huang, Ying Li, Liling Li

palgrave
macmillan

Ruo Si
Tsinghua University
Beijing, China

ISBN 978-981-16-5343-8 ISBN 978-981-16-5344-5 (eBook)
https://doi.org/10.1007/978-981-16-5344-5

This Palgrave Macmillan imprint is published by the registered company Springer Nature Singapore Pte Ltd.
The registered company address is: 152 Beach Road, #21-01/04 Gateway East, Singapore 189721, Singapore

Preface

The past two decades have witnessed the shift from television shopping to livestreaming e-commerce. The origin backgrounds, main advantages and operating of the two business models differ, but in a comparative perspective, it is not difficult to see the coherence of information technology development. From the rise of social media to the popularity of short videos and livestreaming, people's demands for social interaction and information are becoming more and more detailed and diverse.

The COVID-19 pandemic swept through the whole world in 2020, hitting the world economy and changing the employment structure of various countries dramatically. In the long term, economic recovery after the pandemic will last for a long time, and all countries struggle to find a new economic equilibrium. Experiencing rapid development during the pandemic, livestreaming e-commerce is becoming a new economic normal in China. When watching the livestreaming, people not only have fun from interaction, but also engage in economic consumption. For hosts, they earn their living through livestreaming e-commerce. A large number of ordinary people from the lower and middle classes have become hosts and the improvement of their lives demonstrates technological empowerment. In addition to empowering individuals, livestreaming e-commerce also plays an important role in poverty alleviation, transmission of intangible cultural heritages and regional development.

This work consists of five chapters and aims to present a complete landscape of China's livestreaming e-commerce industry. The first chapter introduces the industry's evolvement, comparing livestreaming e-commerce with traditional television shopping to analyse its innovation. The second chapter gives a comprehensive introduction to the technical and social environment of livestreaming e-commerce as well as government policies and regulations concerning the industry. The third chapter analyses influencers' marketing methodology in e-commerce livestreaming through deep interpretation of some phenomenal hosts' success stories. The fourth chapter concentrates on the development and strategy principles of main livestreaming e-commerce platforms in China, which include not only typical e-commerce-oriented platforms like Taobao, but also social networking platforms represented by TikTok and Kwai. In the end, the fifth chapter analyses potential risks of livestreaming e-commerce, which may come from host obligations, legal relationships between MCN agencies and hosts, as well as product selection. Aside from proposing some solutions to the existing problems, this chapter also tries to make objective predictions about the development trends of livestreaming e-commerce in the post-pandemic era, which concern industry standardisation, coordinate development with more industries, more diversified professional backgrounds of livestreamers, market expansion boosted by the long tail effect and digital operation management. We sincerely hope that our present work will provide a reference for future studies on China's livestreaming e-commerce industry.

Beijing, China Ruo Si

Contents

List of Figures

Chapter 2

List of Tables

Author Profile

Si Ruo, Ph.D./Associate Professor (Tenure Track), Doctoral Supervisor

Research Interests

Film and TV Industry
Internet Audio-visual Content
Cultural Tourism Industry

Educational Background

Ph.D. in Humanity, Hong Kong Baptist University, 2007
M.A., Tsinghua University, 2004
B.A., Shandong University, 2001

Working Experience

2018~now	Tsinghua University, School of Journalism and Communication, Associate Professor (Tenure Track), Doctoral Supervisor
2016~2018	Communication University of China, School of Theater, Film and Television, Professor
2011~2016	Communication University of China, School of Theater, Film and Television, Associate Professor

2013~2016	Postdoctoral Fellow, Tsinghua University and Radio and Television Administration of Shandong Province
2011	University of Southern California, School of Cinematic Arts, Visiting Scholar
2007~2011	Communication University of China, School of Theater, Film and Television, Lecturer
2009	China Education Television, Temporary Position

Current Courses

Audio-visual Language

Film and Television Management

Short Drama Film Workshop

Service

Professional Committee of Film Industry and Management of Chinese Collegial Association for Visual Art, Secretary General/Council Member

Theory and Review Committee of China Film Association, Council Member

Beijing Film Association, Member

Sil-Metropole Organization Ltd., Senior Adviser

Publications

1. Research on the Construction of Chinese Film and Television Industrialization System, Social Sciences Academic Press (China), 2020.
2. Blue Book on Film and Television—Development Report of China's Film and Television Industry (2020), Social Sciences Academic Press (China), 2020.
3. Cultural Tourism Blue Book—Report on the Development of China's Cultural Tourism Industry (2019), Social Sciences Academic Press (China), 2019.
4. Internet Audio-Visual Blue Book—Report on the Development of China's Internet Audio-Visual Industry (2019), Social Sciences Academic Press (China), 2019.
5. Legal Practice and Business of Film and Television in China, China Film Press, 2017.

Journal Articles

1. Research on the Development and Future Trend of Chinese Online Movies, *Film Art*, 2020.4;
2. Construction of Multiple Experiences: Prediction of the Development Trend of China's Film Industry in the 2020 Pandemic, *Journal of Beijing Film Academy*, 2020.4;
3. Research on the Developing Path of Domestic Online Film Critics in Recent Years, *Contemporary Cinema*, 2020.3;
4. Between Art and Commerce: The Current Situation of the Dissemination of French Films in China Under the Perspective of Cultural Discount from 2009 to 2018, *Journal of Beijing Film Academy*, 2009.12;
5. Promote Short Video Content Upgraded, Empower Mainstream Culture Dissemination, *Moder Audio-Video Arts*, 2019.8;
6. The Enlightenment of Short Video Development to TV Program Innovation, *China Radio and TV Academic Journal*, 2019.8;
7. Research on the Mode Innovation of Documentary Audio-Visual Works in the Era of Media Convergence, *Modern Communication*, 2019.3;
8. Methods and Paths of Value Evaluation of Film Copyright, *Modern Publishing*, 2019.1;
9. The Path to Integrative Development of Film, TV and Cultural Tourism, *Modern Audio-Video Arts*, 2018.12;
10. The Investment Opportunity Analysis of Urban Cinemas: A Case Study of Dezhou, *Shandong, Contemporary Cinema*, 2018.11.

Current Research Grants

1. Research on the Construction of Chinese Film and Television Industrialization System, Supported by The National Social Science Fund of China as the Post-funded Project;
2. Research on Risk Assessment and Risk Control of Film Project Based on Big Data, Supported by National Radio and Television Administration Social Science as the Major Project;
3. Research on Risk Assessment and Risk Control System of Movies and TV Series Based on Big Data, Supported by Social Science Fund of Beijing.

Works of Art

1. The Grandmaster (Producer Assistant)
2. Mr. Cinema (Planner)
3. The Legend of North Wei Dynasty (Producer Assistant)
4. Qianye and Changsheng (Planner and Producer)
5. The Journey to The Throne (Co-producer)
6. The Royal Guard (Chief Screenwriter)

Honors and Rewards

1. The First Prize of Research Report by Chinese Collegial Association for Visual Art (2018);
2. The First Prize of Research Report by Chinese Collegial Association for Visual Art (2017);
3. The Second Prize of Media Management Research in the 14th National Radio, Film and Television Academic Papers Selection (2016);
4. The Excellent Scientific Research Achievement Award of Communication University of China (2016);
5. "Excellent Young and Middle-aged Teacher Prize" of Communication University of China (2013);
6. The 10th Excellent Scientific Research Achievement Award of Communication University of China (2012);
7. Teaching Contribution Award of School of Theater, Film and Television, Communication University of China (2011);
8. Teaching Quality Award of School of Theater, Film and Television Arts, Communication University of China (2010);
9. Excellent Worker of the Year of Communication University of China (2009).

Introduction

Since its inception in 2016, livestreaming e-commerce has been gaining popularity among the capital market and the public. The success of this business model has been driven by a combination of multiple factors such as favourable policies, technological innovation and the growth of new social media.

The pandemic in 2020 has made livestreaming e-commerce with both practical and entertainment characteristics an attractive option for consumers, stimulating market demand worth trillions of yuan, and the potential huge incremental space will be a long-term development trend of livestreaming e-commerce. Focusing more on the continuous connection between hosts and viewers as well as the immersive participation of the viewers, livestreaming e-commerce has created a new media spectacle in the age of mobile communication.

Based on theories of communication, semiotics, sociology and media economics, this work tries to present a complete landscape of China's livestreaming e-commerce industry from an interdisciplinary perspective. Following the underlying logic of "people, products and fields", this work systematically analyses the evolution process and development background of China's livestreaming e-commerce, providing introduction to main livestreaming e-commerce platforms in China and influencers' marketing methodology. However, the work also analyses potential industrial risks and predicts the development trends of livestreaming e-commerce in the post-pandemic era from the aspects of supply chain optimisation, coordinated industry development, long tail marketing, hosts' professional backgrounds and digital operation management.

Since 2016, livestreaming e-commerce has won the favour of the market and the public as a new business model, due to multiple factors such as government incentive, technological progress, Internet traffic support, shopping experience upgrades and the advancement of social network.[1] Livestreaming e-commerce, featured with a sense of "instant fulfilment" it rarely fails to provides, now is deemed as an attractive and reasonable shopping way, more than offline shopping in which the fulfilment of needs is delayed, thus generating uncertainty, especially under the consistent, worldwide influence of the COVID-19 pandemic. For many Chinese, livestreaming e-commerce that is both practical and diverting has become the first option of daily entertainment. Those who are used to and in need of livestreaming e-commerce already exceeded billions, and the number is still rising. Under the changing media environment in the epidemic, livestreaming e-commerce gains new features every now and then as a channel connecting with the public. For instance, now, it is a distinguishing feature of livestreams on mobile that a consistent interaction between hosts and audience, or in other words, audience's participation and feeling of immersion are never absent if profit is expected. This may reflect the big picture of the varying media ecosystem, which lays emphasis on

[1] Dong Jie, Wang Yijie, "Shaping Mechanisms of Youth Attention: Take TikTok as an Example", *China Youth Study*, February 2020.

storytelling, performance and novelty. This book analyses the process of television home shopping evolving to short video shopping, and that of short video shopping to livestreaming e-commerce. The analyses are established on interdisciplinary theories covering semiology, sociology, media economics and communication studies, based on the underlying logic of "people, product and scene", in the hope of finding the key elements of ensuring the success of promotional products in livestreams, and explaining why such products can generate sustainable market value. In the meantime, we will conduct a thorough exploration in risk control in the livestream industry, which concerns with commercial risks and public relations crises alike, to provide suggestions for avoiding risks that are either incidental or somehow inevitable. In the five chapters, multiple dimensions will be taken into discussion, such as livestream host's obligations and preset personas, the legal relationship between hosts and MCN (Multi-Channel Network) organisations, political restrictions on livestream content, rules of product supply and selection, all in the context of livestreaming e-commerce. Furthermore, to predict the future of livestreaming e-commerce as a sunrise industry, a series of marketing methods are to be discussed in this book as well, including supply chain management, long tail marketing operation, decentralisation of influencer marketing, digital operations, etc., given the fact the Chinese market system is growing more digitalised and intellectual day-to-day.

CHAPTER 1

The Evolvement of Livestreaming E-Commerce

Abstract This chapter introduces the evolvement of livestreaming e-commerce in chronological order. Considering television home shopping is the antecedent of livestreaming e-commerce, this chapter analyses the leading networks in the Chinese television shopping industry such as Happigo, CNRmall and Huanteng Shopping. Compared with television shopping, livestreaming e-commerce is more attractive to young people with scenarised marketing models, humanised host performance, flexible and intelligent supply chain. This chapter also gives a brief introduction to short video industry's rising, which symbolises the dawn of livestreaming e-commerce. From brands setting up official accounts and conducting short video marketing, to users making purchases through links switching to e-commerce apps, short video platforms have achieved a closed-loop connecting content to e-commerce.

Keywords Television shopping · Short videos · Social attention resources · Traffic accumulation

R. Si, *China Livestreaming E-commerce Industry Insights*,
https://doi.org/10.1007/978-981-16-5344-5_1

1 The Antecedent: Television Home Shopping

1.1 The Rise of Television Home Shopping

Television home shopping is a shopping mode using television as the medium to cultivate customer base and select products according to customers need, and then sell products on television channels.[1] Customers gathered by television shopping channels are brought into a virtualised shopping scene that seemingly offers ideal products with preferable prices, thus leading to group consumption. Television home shopping may build and maintain strong customer loyalty, offering customers irregular temporal and spatial shopping experiences, which greatly differentiates it from physical shopping offline.

The rise of television home shopping can be tracked back to 1982. At the beginning, the new marketing model was operated mainly by specialised corporations with few exceptions worldwide. The first television home shopping company—Home Shopping Network—was born in the United States and known by their innovative online stores and contact-free shopping process that were wildly accepted as soon as they were introduced to the public. The popularity led to a rapid growth of market size, while the new model was defied as "the third revolution in the retail industry". At the time when it was newly born, television home shopping was the primary method to conduct online retail and interactive marketing. Later, it evolved into a new form based on TV and the Internet complementing each other, which gave rise to a series of networks specialising in televised and Internet home shopping like QVC, as in Quality Value Convenience.

The first televised home shopping programme on the Chinese mainland was produced in 1992 by Guangdong Pearl River Channel, which is named "Essences of Beauty: The TV Outlet". It is known as the beginning of Mainland China's television home shopping industry. At this point, television home shopping in China was only starting to get off the ground, trying to be acquainted with the market environment. The market size was small and the large-scale development was yet to come. The year 1996 was monumental for China's television home shopping industry, as BTV (Beijing TV Station) opened the first professional TV

[1] Duan Guanghong, "Professionalisation of Televised Shopping Hosts", *Media Forum*, June 2020.

shopping channel on Chinese mainland, marking the beginning of a new era. Then, in 1999, ET Mall, the first televised shopping network in Taiwan Province was established and soon became a trendsetter in the industry.

As a dominant device for information output at the time, television was effective on gathering public attention and providing amusement in the audience's everyday life. Through it, television home shopping created an alternative scene for traditional retailers, which proved to be competent to rise conversion rates and advertising effects. Expert interviews, vigorous shopping guides and live product trails labelled the time of television home shopping. "It only cost you 998 (RMB), just pick up the phone and go for it! Last ten batches! We only have ten batches left! You sure will be regret if you miss it!" The verbal tricks and magical power of charm are highly distinctive, very much resembling that of the modern-day commercial livestream hosts' common wording, such as "Oh my God! Go for it, just go for it! You will end up empty handed if you hesitate!", a repeating pattern used by Li Jiaqi, one of the most well-known Chinese livestream hosts.

It has been more than twenty years since television home shopping set foot in the Chinese market, from TV shopping channels to TV-Internet-blended advertising, from monochrome to digital colour. In those years, television's influence and imagination-stimulating power over the audience stayed incomparable. A television screen indicated the opening boundary between reality and imagination, as it created an idealised, dreamlike world, where life is full of colour and materially abundant, which is exactly what the audience desired. Back then, audience's dependence on television was not limited to watching, but strongly reflected in the purchasing behaviours when they participated in television home shopping.

1.2 The Leading Networks in the Chinese Television Shopping Industry

Today, television home shopping still has users in China, despite the extreme popularity of livestreaming e-commerce. Since it deeply relies on shopping channels and multichannel distributing systems, the television shopping channels in China are relatively dispersive, judging by the regional distribution and broadcasting modes. The concentration rate is by no means high, as half of the market is occupied by seven to eight televised shopping corporations. The audience's attention, on the other hand, is highly concentrated, as over 90% of TV shopping consumers only make purchases on one channel, while 80% of the purchases are made on merely a few channels. On the other hand, Chinese TV shopping users are mainly aged from fifty to sixty, who were born in 1960s or 1970s. Consequently, the average price of television-promoted merchandise is relatively high, as the customers' purchasing power focuses mainly on healthcare products that are relatively easy to attract senior citizens and female audience who value physical health, youthful appearance and have money to spare. In fact, females and senior citizens in good economic conditions have always been the core users of television home shopping, who contributed the most to the industry's past glory.

The national, provincial and municipal television shopping channels in China are listed as follows:

National channels

1. CCTV Home Shopping of China Central Television
2. CNRmall of China National Radio
3. Global Home Shopping (GHS) of China Radio International
4. JiaJia Mall of Anhui Broadcasting Corporation
5. Happigo of Hunan Broadcasting System
6. UGO of Shanxi Radio and Television Station
7. SSGO of Chongqing Broadcasting Group
8. Jiayou Home Shopping of Guizhou Broadcasting and Television Station
9. FS Shopping of Jiangxi Radio and TV Station

Provincial channels

1. Aijia Home Shopping of Beijing Broadcasting Corporation
2. Yijia Home Shopping of Liaoning Radio and TV Station
3. Swan Shopping of Harbin Broadcasting and TV Station
4. OCJ of Shanghai Media Group
5. Jiangsu Enjoy Shopping
6. Jujia shopping (Lepai Home Shopping) of Shandong Radio and TV Station
7. Lejia Home Shopping of Shaanxi Broadcasting Corporation

8. Meijia Home Shopping of Hubei Media Group
9. Kaixin Home Shopping of Guangdong South Media Corporation (SMC)
10. Star Shopping Channel of Sichuan Radio and Television Station
11. Haoyigou (Best 1 TV Shopping Mall) of Zhejiang Radio and Television Station
12. Family Shopping of Taiyuan Radio and Television Station
13. Consumer Guide of Wuhan Broadcasting and Television Station
14. Eachome Shopping of Shenzhen TV Station
15. Everyday Shopping of Chengdu Radio and Television Station

Municipal channels

1. Jiaxi Shopping of Fuzhou Broadcasting and Television Station
2. Quanxin Shopping of Xiamen TV Station
3. The Home Shopping channel of Guangzhou Broadcasting Network
4. Legou Shopping of Xi'an Broadcasting Corporation
5. Shenshi Shopping of Shenyang Radio and TV Station
6. Letian Shopping of Dalian Radio and TV Station

Non-governmental channels

1. Shanghai Seven Star Shopping
2. Shanghai Acorn International
3. Guangdong Hongshenggou
4. Beijing Moral International

The home shopping channels in China can be divided into three "echelons". The first echelon includes Happigo, OCJ, CNRmall, Yijia Home Shopping, UGO, Enjoy Shopping, Best 1 TV Shopping Mall, Eachome Shopping, Jiayou Home Shopping, CCTV Home Shopping and JiaJia Mall. The second echelon consists of nine channels including TVSN, U-You Shopping, Trend Shopping (LCTV 8), Meijia Home Shopping, Lepai Shopping, Fashion TV Shopping, Lejia Home Shopping, Huanteng Shopping and GS Home Shopping. The third echelon has Star Shopping

Channel, Happy Music Shopping, Tiantian Sunshine Shopping, U-Mall, Quanxin Shopping, etc.

Happigo

Among all the channels mentioned, Happigo is of typical significance and head effects of the new generation of television home shopping. Jointly established by Hunan Golden Eagle Broadcasting System and Hunan Satellite TV, it is symbolic for being the first large modern corporation specialising in televised home shopping in Mainland China, formed at the turning point of the industry. Soon after established, the company's business expanded rapidly and covered a large area across the country from Yangtze River Delta to Pearl River Delta, due to the popularity of digital TV in the developed cities. This gave Happigo a comprehensive advantage in the market, which helped it built up the nationwide monopoly of digital television home shopping soon after.

When the Internet started to gain popularity in China, starting its industrial practice, a competition emerged between Internet shopping and television home shopping. Facing the challenge, leading channels like Happigo first made their respond. Among the local TV stations, Hunan Broadcasting System was the earliest to upgrade televised shopping service. Cooperating with Taobao in 2010, Hunan Satellite TV repackaged Happigo, aiming to secure a place in the market environment altered by the flourishing Internet. The company opened a customised shopping channel on Taobao, selling popular TV shows and series as their staple. This stimulated the offline purchasing power and then transferred it into Internet traffic, putting up an energetic e-commerce platform that linked with Happigo. It is a kind of cycle operation that makes high profit by investing capital and creative ideas in the new business model that blended the TV industry and physical retail, and then feeds the gained profit back to the TV shopping channel, making new profit that will be used at the beginning of a new cycle. The upgrade proved to be a success, helped Happigo win a lot of public praise, market profit and positive reputation, and even saved the industry from the tremendous impact of the Internet as it was widely applied later.

CNRmall

CNRmall is a television home shopping channel operated by China National Radio (CNR), launched on June 1, 2010, in Beijing and Tianjin.

It is the eighth national home shopping channel opened in Mainland China issued by National Radio and Television Administration,[2] at first using television as primary medium, playing the role of adhesive to glue together the traditional advertising media and the retail industry, which is also an outcome of the media industrialisation. Later, CNRmall's business scope extended to Internet shopping, catalogue shopping and mobile TV shopping. As an omni-media integration, CNRmall shows that television home shopping still has some vitality to overlook the whole picture of the media industry.

OCJ

To seize the opportunity in the media industrialisation, Shanghai Media Group (SMG) joined hands with CJ Group of Korea and founded Oriental CG (OCG), a transnational corporation specialising in television home shopping. OCG's first TV shopping trail was launched in April 2004 on China Drama Channel of Dragon TV, the satellite television section of SMG. 350 families in Shanghai were granted access to the trail. Afterwards, OCG's television shopping service extended widely, linking with cable TV channels, websites and radio broadcasts, with an overall upgrade regarding product selection, testing, delivery and after-sales, seeking for more possibilities. In the meantime, the company improved their shopping websites and shopping guide service, as well as launched an online shopping mall, which contained all the product information that went concurrently with their TV shopping channel. From then on, OCG's customers could search for product instructions, order and preorder what they like, check messages of ordering, delivery and shopping points, all on the Internet, in many ways of payment such as paying online, cash on delivery and swiping a card on a POS terminal. By then, OCG's online shopping mall was featured with the novelty of digital stores and the pre-existed supply chain, though it still relied on traditional media to complete online conversion. It was the time when the embryo of e-commerce was cultivated.

[2] "CNR's Televised Home Shopping Channel Is Coming", released by Xinhuanet on June 4, 2010. http://www.cctv.com/cctvsurvey/special/01/20100604/101858.shtml.

Jujia Shopping (Lepai Home Shopping)

Jujia Shopping (Lepai Home Shopping) is a televised shopping channel founded by Shandong Radio and TV Media Group and Lepai Business Corporation, which is the only shopping channel in Shandong Province issued by National Radio and Television Administration of China, known for open and transparent product selection, customised product display and real-time payment. At first, Jujia Shopping offered 6.5 hours of live shopping programmes per day, while recorded programmes took up the rest of the time. Later, 24-hour live shopping programmes were gradually applied.

Haoyigou (Best 1 TV Shopping Mall)

Haoyigou, namely Best 1 TV Shopping Mall, was a televised home shopping company founded by Zhejiang Radio and Television Station and Zhejiang Radio and TV Group, with Eastern Multimedia Group of Taiwan taking part in the operation. Haoyigou was born in December 22, 2006, and of the expectation to build a zero-store online supermall that could be widely accessed by domestic customers, so that "Easy and good buy, easy and good life" was made a featured slogan.

To implement their customer-oriented strategy, Haoyigou tried to shorten the shopping process as well as broaden the entry for customers by constructing a zero-store B2C (Business to Customer) highway using cable TV channels, product catalogues and websites as media. To achieve so, it also introduced from abroad advanced shopping information management systems, put a 20,000m^2 automatic warehouse into service, trained 300 customer service agents, executed a CRM (Customer Relationship Management) programme and reached cooperation with EMS, China Postal Express and Logistics' express mail service. Moreover, to ensure a stable audience rating, the company has been offering 6.5 hours of live shopping programmes per day in each of the ten areas of the studio, expecting to satisfy the multifarious needs of the widely reached customers.

Huanteng Shopping

Huanteng Shopping is a televised shopping channel operated by Business Information Channel of Henan Broadcasting System. It is a rather down-to-earth shopping channel, since most of the merchandise promoted on the channel could be found in the local malls also, and that the company's strategic principle was mainly "small profits and quick turnover". Huanteng's another advantage is that its business credit is backed by Henan Broadcasting System, who makes Huanteng's product quality seemingly more reassuring due to their government background.

Huanteng shopping's overall operation system is divided into a series of self-contained modules, including strict commodity selection, programme production, telephone call centre operation, logistics and after-sales service. It is also an integration of the parent company's marketing resources in the media industry. The company claims that they aim to offer "good products, good prices and good service", and once was praised as "a cheap department store in the sky, a shopping mall soaring high". Above all, however, it was a vessel though which Henan Broadcasting System matched into the modern e-commerce industry and achieved a large-scale commercialisation.

2 From Television Home Shopping to Livestreaming E-Commerce

History always repeats itself in a surprising way. Without exception, the rise and decline of every television home shopping channel, the whole industry's evolvement and decay, and today's prosperity of livestreaming e-commerce are crucially relevant to the loyalty of customers established in a closed-loop process of purchase. Ever since the Internet rose and acquiring market information became easier, more and more customers were seen changing into human advertisements, willingly sharing their shopping experiences and feelings by words with their families and acquaintances, which was how the earliest user groups and consumption communities were formed, vertical with certain products whose reputation was sound in certain social circles. Furthermore, the sharers continued to draw attention of more consumers and simultaneously enhanced the dissemination effect of consumer behaviours. At the time when livestreaming e-commerce came, Internet traffic's flowability was already strong, striking people with successions of storms that come and go in haste, causing information explosions and a serious lack of concentration. Resultantly, it was an ordinary acquaintance people tend to trust rather than some invisible company hiding behind TV screens. So exponentially, the acquaintance-driven, word-of-mouth dissemination hastened the drawing of traffic into commercial livestreams conducted by acquaintance-like hosts, who fully comprehended the customers' needs, behaved in a way only a family or a friend would, and on top of that, offered highly preferable discounts seemingly nowhere else to be found. As time went on, however, merely depending on low prices appeared to be no more enough, since plenty of new factors, such as stronger user interaction, more explicit user data and a wider variety of on-platform traffic, each of them now has a role to play.

2.1 Age and Region Structures

Most often, a TV shopping channel uses TV presenters to promote merchandise in four steps, which in turn are foreshadowing, exposing, pricing and inciting, extremely efficient to inflame elder consumers' desire to purchase. The senior citizens have proved to be the most active users of television home shopping, but the chances they provide repeat business are very small. According to AgeClub, a Chinese data corporation specialising in Internet data statistics, 77% of the Chinese elder people living in the first-tier cities who have experienced television home shopping choose not to rebuy, and the rate of rebuying is merely 20–30%, which shows a serious possibility of losing customers. Television home shopping was born in the time of limited choices of media and hardly any fission-communication, while the strongest purchasing power was owned by those born in the 1960s or the 1970s, rather than those born in 1990s or after the millennium. The younger generation, however, have shown more eagerness to follow new fashion trends and easier to cognise and accept novelties. Inherently, they are prospective fans of newborn IPs that focus on entertaining and mind-blowing. With the young generation being the most vertical users, livestreaming e-commerce is naturally of strong user penetration and effective communication. In the past few years, China's livestreaming e-commerce has saw a downtrend of average user age and a rising popularity in the non-first-tier cities, meaning a good many of the Chinese younger generation living in less developed cities and small towns are keen on filling their leisure time with watching commercial livestreams, which is quite the opposite of television home shopping's user structure in the aspects of age and region.

2.2 Traditional and Scenarised Marketing Models

Television home shopping heavily relies on but one marketing model, namely, of course, television advertising. As a market model, it is rather traditional with almost none host-audience real-time interaction, though effective when it meets customers' preference for low prices. Traditional television advertising gives audience product information in a straightforward and monotonous way, by today's standards. It depends on merchants paying television channels handsomely for the prime time to achieve a satisfying audience rating. By comparison, today's livestreaming e-commerce shows a multi-layered improvement in the respect that it is highly humanised and scenarised. In a commercial livestream, the host's seemingly personal commendation on a product effectively conceals the livestream's commercial nature and thus avoids audience's antipathy towards advertising, which, on the other hand, highly demands the host's skill and experience of performance. In a commercial livestream that lasts three to four hours, a large number and variety of products are to promote, making it a necessity that the host spends time and energy in advance comprehending each product's nature in all the respects, such as function, price and user structure. Only then may the host carry out passionate, eloquent speeches mingling with their own understanding and user experience, to bring the sales well up. As a matter of fact, most occasionally here, it is not a high-quality product that affects audience's expectation, but a product that remarkably spreads and disperses in the market. Therefore, for those who participate in livestreaming e-commerce, it is a must to integrate multiple platforms, including that of e-commerce, short videos and social networking, to draw Internet traffic from a vaster area and achieve a broad-based communication.

In the meantime, the scene of a commercial livestream is highly alterable, depending on the team's choose of marketing models. Were the scene of a commercial livestream substantial in content and successful in replacing bare, straightforward advertisements with the host's entertaining, acquaintance-like performance, it is appealing to the audience and effective on inducing them to make purchase decisions.

The following Table 1 shows several marketing models of livestreaming e-commerce that are commonly used.

Table 1 This chart mainly illustrates the diverse marketing models of livestreaming e-commerce

Marketing models of livestreaming e-commerce	
Models	*Basic features*
Sec-kill	In this model, host's popularity and marketing performance in the past decide if he/she has a say in setting prices when negotiating with the suppliers. If host is good at bargaining, preferable prices much lower than original ones may be possible, so are a considerable amount of instant purchase (called "sec-kill" by Chinese) when livestreaming. This also gives audience an impression that they will keep getting satisfying discounts as long as they are loyal fans
Celebrity-oriented	Also known as KOL-oriented. Host is believed to be a key opinion leader dominating a certain area of expertise, thus competent to exert considerable influence on his/her fans and random audience alike
Physical store livestreaming	Host set livestream scenes in physical stores, recommending products one by one
Production base walk-streaming	Host chooses a production base as livestream scene, where promoted products are originally manufactured, and walks around in the base when livestreaming, showing it to audience. Usually, host must visit the base in advance to make product selection, getting to know material sources, quality details and after-sales service

(continued)

"Give me a place to stand and I will move the Earth", said Archimedes as we know. The pivot point used to "move the Earth" can be regarded as an all-purpose tipping point. Should it fit with a certain possibility, new sparks will be spurred. In the time of digital media integrating, it is but the sense of immersion that plays the role of the pivot point for livestreaming e-commerce to "move the Earth". Through transboundary

Table 1 (continued)

Marketing models of livestreaming e-commerce

Models	*Basic features*
Raw material livestreaming	Host conducts a livestream where the raw materials of promoted products are originally supplied, to emphasise that quality materials guarantee quality products
Customisation	Host and his/her team are either ODMs (original design manufacturers) or OEMs (original equipment manufacturers), who supply specially designed products based on audience's certain needs. This model is featured with customisation and a host-owned supply chain. Product selection is relatively strict
Price cutting	Normally applied in livestreams selling luxuries and rare products. Depending on product functions and features, host bargains with supplier after original price is set, aiming at a maximum discount
Overseas shopping livestreaming	Host goes abroad and livestreams as an overseas purchasing agent. The scene shifts and alters as host travels, providing domestic audience with a sense of immersion. This model naturally demands an overseas supply chain
Expert service	Best for creating an atmosphere of suspense and competition, suitable for commercial activities of gambling nature, such as cutting stones apart for jade or opening oysters for pearls
Rush-to-buy	This model is designed to increase fans' purchasing speed, making them rivals for promoted merchandise

convergence of culture and technology, it breaks the limit of traditional consumption scenes and outputs, creative ideas of storytelling and brand marketing. On the evening of June 15, 2020, Taobao's Tmall joins hands with SMGLive (Shanghai Media Group Live) and Punchdrunk, a British forerunner of immersive theatre who created *Sleep No More*, a typical immersive art show in Shanghai, to put up a theatre-like, marketing-oriented show, filled with the sense of immersion. In the show, the band

Mr. Miss acted as a time travel guide, leading the audience back to The Mackinnon Hotel in 1936 while providing the immersive sense of time travelling as the modern time seamlessly merged with the old. The jazz they played contained in the lyrics the selling points of twenty products, each with an old story behind it and a live performance on the stage. With music as vessels to express selling points, the immersive theatre set a comfortable pace for that night's livestream e-commerce while it inspired the audience's curiosity of the novelties they witnessed. It was a new tactic for livestreaming e-commerce and an avant-garde experiment, which will most likely become a new element of the livestream industry as it brings the audience fresh, even an enjoyably bizarre shopping experience. Surely, there can be more music and stories like those that blend imaginations, creativities and marketing strategies, and that unify brand concepts, product features and business perspectives.

2.3 Host Performance: from Exaggerated to Humanised

Hou Xingzu, CMO of Rosdenton Taiwan and a famous, leather-lunged presenter, used to be a label of the exaggerated performance style in the time of television home shopping. Typical as Hou, television home shopping hosts in the early time usually strived to be extremely quick of tongue to arouse competition among audience, as well as make themselves indispensable out of selling efficiency. TV shopping programmes created in this way are not so far from today's commercial livestreams. Hou was known as the "No.1 screamer on satellite TV", who in his time roared himself hoarse with improvised expressions on his face and figures of speech for promotion that later were deemed as a fashion and even made television home shopping a kind of phenomenal pop culture. After Hou, television home shopping turned to injecting into commodities' storytelling elements, for purpose of lively proving product functions to be convincing, thus to maximise audience's desire to purchase. This marketing model went down a certain period and shaped the early style of Chinese television home shopping in general. It even made TV hosts like Hou Xingzu objects of academic study.

Not earlier than 2016 has livestreaming e-commerce met its flourishment. For a livestreaming e-commerce platform, the basis method to attracting Internet traffic is the platform supports hosts with different resources depending on their marketing performances; hosts are subordinate to traffic, defined and evaluated by the latter. Also, based on algorithmic modelling, the platform gathers data of revenue, audience measurement and so on, which are used to measure hosts' general competitiveness. Some hosts started their career as shopping guides offline and increased the number of customers in a long run, from one to dozens, then from dozens to hundreds, thousands and even millions. Such hosts, therefore, are rather sensitive about numbers of customers, even if they already have in their livestreaming room billions of fans. They clearly know that more fans mean more responsibilities, and more dangers if they fell.

As the basis method is still functional today, words and speeches used by hosts in their livestreams have become a kind of instrumentalised symbol, by which the hosts are labelled, represented and even self-excited when doing livestreams, enthusiastic to control fans' mood as well as their own. This helps the hosts build a close relationship with their fans in long-term interactions, which the hosts tend to call friendship that brings them considerable amount of traffic as an overall advantage. Such being the case, livestreaming hosts nowadays focus more on humanising their performance when livestreaming, in many ways such as adjusting their manners of speaking, preset personas and marketing logics. Livestream e-commerce now has developed a clear orientation, as audience have shown that they are in livestreaming rooms to make purchases rather than to spend time on chit-chat. This has been realised by many hosts, hence the balance between self-expression and marketing performance, and their confidence and unhurried manner as they keep practising in the new way of marketing.

On July 6, 2020, China's Ministry of Human Resources and Social Security cooperated with State Administration for Market Regulation and National Bureau of Statistics, and announced nine new occupations including livestreaming e-commerce. After that, hosts of commercial livestreams are formally defied as "livestreaming salespersons". Some top-notch hosts however, like Viya and Li Jiaqi, prefer to address themselves as "Internet marketers", a title they consider to be more precise and technical, which refers to "practitioners who work on digital platforms, selling and promoting products manufactured and supplied by legal companies, with the aid of the Internet's interactivity and communication credibility", as they described it. They claim that their wish is to energise the brands they promote as well as to make clear plans of how to energise them and, in the meantime, how to express themselves as individuals, which is also the reason why they explore their profession multi-dimensionally and make efforts to increase their values, in the eyes of the public and business partners alike.

2.4 *Supply Chain: from Monotonous and Disordering to Flexible and Intelligent*

The way of forging a supply chain in the time of television home shopping was rather monotonous, as marketing models of every platform showed a lack of change, and the follow-up supply often suffered from disorder in every link of supply control and management, including storage, logistics and distribution. Television home shopping channels tended to aim at pennywise and less educated customers who lived in undeveloped towns and villages where information dissemination was quite limited. As a result, it was common to see a series of problems such as complaint bombing, order overflowing, stockout, distribution breaking off and fakery. In livestreaming e-commerce, on the other hand, supply of products is the most important part of the market system. The infrastructure of livestreaming e-commerce, including payment, distribution and platform construction, is more practical than that of television home shopping. Moreover, actuated by new technologies like big data mining and cloud computing, supply chain of livestreaming e-commerce has become more flexible and intelligent. Influenced by the COVID-19 epidemic, unexpected changes of market condition occur now and then and the supply chain must react quickly to avoid breaking off. For the livestreaming e-commerce industry, improving supply chain's flexibility has become a general strategic principle in the changeful situation. Now, it is a normalcy that livestreaming e-commerce practitioners estimate audience's potential needs, portray accurate user structures, introduce big data analysis into supply chain management and give impetus to its technical upgrade, all with the aid of advanced data analytic models. Taking Viya's e-commerce team as an example, there are five hundred employees in the team and more than 60% of them take part in organising Viya's livestreams, who work together with Viya to carry out product selection mainly complying with three rules. The first rule is to provide custom-made commodities that fulfil the needs of fans, with the help of information gathered from livestreaming chats of Viya and her fans. The second rule is that the host runs on herself a live trail of product before her fans, using her own user experience to make her recommendation convincing. And the third rule, lastly, is that the team submit to the host an evaluation of product's popularity, for the host to make final choices among the products selected and evaluated by them in advance.

There is a re-upgrade in this procedure of product selection, shown by that it is no longer only the host's personal feelings or preference that decides whether a product is to be put on a livestream, but also customers' needs and the team's suggestions. This is more obvious in the selection of edible, which demands the team to do taste tests repeatedly and operate voting and scoring on social media, or to conduct surveys of raw material origins to confirm if standardisation and acceptable quality are reached. This re-upgrade of selection is valued much by Li Jiaqi, whose quality control team consists of five employees, all with master's degrees and major in food studies and chemical test, who Li believes make the expression "quality control" more trustworthy. Aside from that, Li puts in each of his livestreams a direct link to customer service to ensure the smooth going of after-sales support, which is rather effective on avoiding complaints and commercial disputes.

Though experimentally, many of the corporations in the lead of the livestreaming e-commerce industry have begun to integrate supply chain upstream, as shown in the following table:

Rank	*Corporation*	*Leading product in e-commerce*	*Supply chain base established*
1	Qian Xun	Apparel	Yes
2	Nars	Apparel	Yes
3	Hakim Unique Group	Apparel	Yes
4	Gome	Apparel	Yes
5	Jitao Veterans	Apparel	Yes
6	Meet Real	Apparel	Yes
7	Fanwei	Apparel	Yes
8	Xiduo	Apparel	No
9	Duohong Veterans	Apparel	No
10	Wenzi Club	Apparel	Yes

Data Source: *Report on Online Investigation of Consumer Satisfaction of Livestreaming E-Commerce*, China Consumers Association, 2020

3 Short Video's Rising: The Dawn of Livestream E-Commerce

3.1 *Influencers of the First Generation: IP Incubation and Traffic Accumulation*

The evolution from short videos to livestreaming e-commerce is a milestone in the history of home shopping. Ever since the Internet technology began to shape the nature of web-born content, the e-commerce industry started to make breakthroughs. The first sign was the transboundary combination of social media and e-commerce. On April 29, 2013, Alibaba Group and Sina Weibo reached a strategic cooperation after the two Internet tycoons formally discussed the issue for 46 times. The lengthy negotiation ended with Alibaba taking a stake in Weibo which cost the former 56.8 million dollars, all invested in the IP incubation of China's first-generation social media influencers, mainly through offering them private Internet traffic. This aroused the first wave of supply chain innovation as well as explored new marketing models of lately socialised e-commerce. Soon after Alibaba's venture, China's first-generation online influencers were produced. Among them, there were some most representative Internet celebrities at that time, such as Eve Zhang (Zhang Dayi), Cherie (Xue Li), Aunty Guan and Momo (Zhang Mofan).

Among the many of their marketing plans, the first choice of the first-generation influencers was a better fan management, which later developed to large-scale community operation. They started with turning the private traffic offered by the platform into huge number of fans and then tried to make the fans stay by providing information they favoured, like recommending makeup tutorial videos or sharing personal emotional experience through pictures and snippets of text. As loyal users accumulated and reached a certain number, they upgraded the accumulation to vast community management. It was then they began to make use of celebrity effect and the burgeoning short videos. Internet celebrities and even film stars were invited to take part in making and spreading the short videos they made, ceaselessly stoking the public's curiosity. The new way of video making that allowed them to film anything they liked with plenty of background music to choose freely was undoubtedly a refreshing attraction and suitable for spreading. Most of the videos made in this way were no longer than 10 seconds, which went quite well with celebrity effect in the process of dissemination. This also made Miaopai, the Internet company who first introduced this new way of video making to Weibo users. Later, Weibo joined hands with Yixia Technology, who soon developed short video applications exclusively for Weibo, making full use of the platform's social networking attribute known for openness and high level of user interaction. Since all the collaborations turned out satisfying so far, Weibo went further and brought Yi Live into partnership, who then built on Weibo an exclusive livestreaming platform. Both Miaopai and Yi Live smoothly got involved in Weibo's massive Internet traffic resources, while the first-generation influencers changed their marketing logic from using illustrated words to applying short videos and livestreams. The experiment of transforming short video e-commerce to livestreaming e-commerce had commenced.

The information given above shows the evolving process of influencer-driven e-commerce, during the time when Weibo dominated China's social networking. Clearly, the influencers' top priority back then was not to make sales as efficiently as possible, but to create multi-dimensional value for their personal IPs, which they intended to exchange for high conversion rate when the time came. As for the platform, the main strategy was to output personal preferences and life styles of the influencers to gather public attention on social network ports, starting from providing a feeling of being an Internet celebrity for the fans to imitate with passion. The common content presented to the fans mainly consisted of photo/video shooting tours overseas, life styles of delicacy and beauty, makeup video tutorials and dressing style recommendations, which fans would find useful and entertaining alike and thus become clung to the influencers and the platform. Consequently, the younger generation's consumption view had been largely altered as they were steered to favour products that were cheaper and promoted by the influencers. It was the influencers' credibility those young Internet inhabitants relied on and, predictably, they were directed to form a close emotional bond with the influencers once the trust was built.

Not long after that, another time of change came as the transition of user habit from PC to mobile was near completion, and WeChat had risen to show its ambition of seizing the market and opened harsh competition with Weibo. At that time, Weibo still held a high ground in the market as its primary accumulation of registered users and visitor volume had reached a considerable amount and the traffic it attracted was seeing a sustainable growth. The platform by then had over 400 million registered users and 42.3 million daily active users on average, with 60% of them visiting the platform on mobile devices. The advertising revenue generated by the mammoth user community once reached 20 million RMB per quarter, according to the third quarter financial report by Sina, Weibo's parent company in November 2012. However, the huge group of enterprise users, namely 200,000 at the time, had severely handicapped the platform's commercial strategies.

In the meantime, Alibaba, who had been assembling small and medium-sized businesses under their roof, managed to accumulate hundreds of millions of reliable consumers. Though the user base was concrete, the Taobao platform under Alibaba's wing had always faced unsatisfactory outcomes in a series of attempts at practising large-scale shopping guide and vast community management. Plenty of social networking platforms including Yahoo Relationship, Lakeside (Hupan), Contact (Laiwang) and some Pinterest-like applications all made efforts to join force with Taobao and hopefully expand their business territories to mobile. And yet they all failed to make themselves phenomenal applications because of negative market responds or their content slighted by the public.

3.2 The Swift Expansion of Short Videos

We are moving from the information age to the conceptual age, as American Futurist Daniel H. Pink said. Pink drew out six right brain functions that he believed were relevant to the conceptual age, which were Design, Story, Symphony, Empathy Play and Meaning.[3] All without exception will be of increasing significance soon. Correspondingly, video makers on China's short video platforms can be classified into six types, specialising respectively in entertainment, artistic performance, emotional guidance, lifestyle recommendation, knowledge popularisation and facial attractiveness, each type of makers having a conceptual cyberspace to settle in. Based on this condition, the users' attention moving from traditional social media to short video platforms is one of the results of the fragmentation of Internet content and the popularity of shooting videos in portrait mode, and also the users' collective choice in the competitive market environment, for videos that are brief and shot in portrait mode

[3] Chen Hedan, You Keke, Zhang Jinwen, "Short Video's Value: Lifestyle, Communication and Consumption", *Communication and Society*, Beijing: Communication University of China Press, 2020.

are regarded by Chinese audience as more lifelike and amiable, full of charm in a special way and easy to involve in their daily lives that can even lead to addiction.

Along with the popularisation of the mobile Internet since the first-generation influencer was produced, the number of mobile users in China rose increasingly, as their content-consumption habit was gradually developed. The corollary was that the popularity of short videos stayed high for a long time, showing no trace of declining, and the Internet traffic was close to saturation. In September 2016, TikTok (Douyin) officially went online domestically and soon became an ideal platform for short videos and one of the largest gathering of Internet traffic in China. The company began to implement their global strategies in August 2017. By now, TikTok has harvested more than 100 million monthly active users overseas in over 150 countries. According to Sensor Tower, an American research firm, TikTok was the most downloaded application for iPhone in the first quarter of 2018, followed by Facebook, YouTube and Instagram. As for the domestic market in the first half of the same year, the number of TikTok users in China had reached 500 million with a rapid growth of the company's market share, shown in the report released by QuestMobile. For the past few years, short video applications such as TikTok and Kwai (Kuaishou) have seen the numbers of downloads and daily active users continuously on the increase, while new platforms like WeSee (Weishi) and Volcano (Huoshan Tiny Video) also made these years a time to flourish, as well as proved themselves viable entertaining alternatives for short video lovers. And considering that users of most short video applications can now make and share UGC (User Generated Content), they are hardly mere receivers any more but also transmitters, who prefer videos of 15 seconds to 1 minute's duration that are more straightforward and filled with newness, wonder and the efficiency to deliver the sense of immersion in limited time and involve audience in the content, with highly simplified audio-visual languages.

3.2.1 *Short Videos' Charms: Realistic Interaction, Free Performance and Collective Identity*

To the rise and popularisation of short videos, opinion leader and celebrity participation gave a strong push. On major short video platforms such as TikTok, the uploaders included not only social elites and professional videographers, but most of the domestic film and television stars also. Taking advantage of the platforms that carry creative content and depending on their entertaining creativity and appeal to the public, the beloved actors and actresses have made themselves vessels for new means of entertainment, interacting with their fans and enriching their personas more effectively and vividly. If we defined Weibo as the first-generation celebrity-driven social media in China, short video platforms have proved to be its ambitious successors that are welcoming a massive wave of celebrity immigration. By the end of June 2020, there had been 2,533 film and television stars who stationed on the TikTok platform and published 126,084 short videos that harvested over 250 billion likes, according to Funji's statistics. It is obvious that TikTok accounts have become one of the most valuable assets among the celebrities' digital resources, even indispensable if they wish to sustain and spread their influence.

Another main reason for short videos' mass attraction is that short video applications are known for their fitness for interaction, and their capability of leading users into an unknown, prodigious world full of excitement and seemingly infinite possibility awaiting. When users enter the digital world anonymously, the boundary between real-life and Internet identity creates a potential for multiple mirroring. As Esther Dyson, an American Internet researcher argued that anonymity, as with a mask, is worn by an individual to reveal his or her true nature rather than to conceal it; in other words, the "mask" allows the wearer to genuinely demonstrate a certain aspect of his or her characters.[4] The users are not merely receiving messages as they tap the screen and immerse themselves in a short video, but also demonstrating part of their real selves freely under a digital scene's cover, enjoying the pleasure of relief as well as deriving a sense of achievement from others' attention and concern, to pursue and achieve self-realisation. Everyone has dreamt to be famous, and the short video platforms have offered ordinary people a chance to perform their daily lives and the feeling of a dream come true. They upload videos that contain whatever they think is interesting, realistic and heartwarming that originates from their daily lives and share them with each of their audience. It is not difficult for videos of this kind to hit the bull's eye of people's concern with their recreational and radiative content that can easily trigger group empathy and awareness of collective

[4] Esther Dyson, *Release 2.0: A Design for Living in the Digital Age*, trans. by Hu Bing, Fan Shenyan, Haikou: Hainan Publishing House, 1998, p. 70.

identity, through fission-communication and group interaction, thus to win audience's hearts and make them more dependent on uploaders.

It is safe to conclude that the three key words for short video culture are fragmentation, performance and interaction.[5] As mentioned in Marxian economics, working has been separated from workers, and workers feel that they are themselves only when they are not working. Working should have been a necessity for humankind to fully achieve physical and spiritual development, and yet for workers, what they obtain from working is never the enjoyment of working, but only what they need to survive. Therefore, every man and woman in a capitalist society has to try retrieving their true selves that they have lost in the process of production, from material and immaterial consumptions alike. From this point of view, it is in fact another instrumentalised myth what those ardently loved short videos have offered the watchers.

Another reason for short videos being so widely appealing is that they have built various kinds of unconventional interactive space, or say "campsites" for various unconventional groups, which makes the applications capable of accommodating users of different social status, occupations and education levels throughout the country. It is rather surprising to see so many people with different backgrounds are willing to share something with each other. We may even say they are rebellious, alternative, unorthodox groups of users, who look as if they always stay underground, living their lives in unusual spaces as hidden branches of the mainstream society, just to secure their own safety. In the video-occupied cyberspace, however, they have chances to meet with like-minded people, put thoughts into actions as a collective and create a bond among each other in the digital world. To them, what short video applications like TikTok and Kwai provide is a responsive platform where their unique cultures can be bred, even if they are considered as marginal groups of Chinese society.

Behind the respect for human instinct, however, short videos are designed with content and topics that are successive, intertwined, integrated, suitable for fission-communication and able to split into countless chains of re-spreading and to improve reposting rate and communication rate largely. In this, we can see a regularity that for a short video social networking application, there is never a one-way path between its

[5] Zhang Yiwu, "Fragmentation, Performance, Interaction", *Globe Times*, July 10, 2020, p. 13.

development and being put on the market. Taking TikTok as an example, the company has implemented a strategy of bidirectional circulation and backflow that interact with and complement each other, which help the application "produce" users while producing content, interaction and topics. What the application has bred are not only short videos favoured by users, but eventually, users who favour the short videos it provides.

In the wake of TikTok's deep exploration of the attention economy, a new way of influencer marketing, namely recommending before selling, has been fully pioneered, and a Pandora's box has been opened.

3.2.2 Short Videos in E-Commerce: Competition for Social Attention Resources

With the innovation and development of media technology, the newly formed media matrix consisting Weibo, WeChat and TikTok has been widely applied to information dissemination. Consequently, the influence of graphics and traditional long videos is weakened by GIF images and short videos. The key to using Weibo, WeChat and short videos to disseminate information is to break through the following three barriers, as in the "repost barrier" (mainly on Weibo), the "social circle barrier" (mainly on WeChat) and the "like barrier" (mainly on short video platforms), which respectively reflect the main attributes of the three media.[6] The focus of Weibo is to encourage users to repost, while as a process from centralisation to decentralisation, information dissemination through WeChat needs to stimulate the proliferation of different social circles. Short videos instead rely heavily on users' likes and algorithmic recommendations to achieve viral marketing. Therefore, the unique features of short video platforms, such as simple operations, fragmented reception, fast dissemination and easy sharing settings facilitate short videos to gain traffic as a precondition for abundant likes, in order to achieve the social effect of millions of audience's appreciations.

Short video platforms characterise the UGC model. Based on creative ideas and specific props, and with the help of personalised recommendation algorithms, short videos that combine entertaining content and livestreaming e-commerce are gradually accepted by users. In fact, short video platforms are constantly building a complete closed-loop covering

[6] Chen Hedan, You Keke, Zhang Jinwen, "Short Video's Value: Lifestyle, Communication and Consumption", *Communication and Society*, Beijing: Communication University of China Press.

content, social interaction and e-commerce, in which users engage in commodity transactions while at the same time devoting their scarce attention. The aggregation of individual attention will form social attention resources of a large scale, guiding the developing direction of collective culture. Unlike individual attention, group attention, as a fundamental resource of human activities, places greater emphasis on the stable and consistent pattern of attention exhibited by human society as a whole to a certain extent. The distribution patterns of social attention resources can be mainly divided into the "temporal distribution pattern", the "spatial distribution pattern", the "social relationship distribution pattern" and the "issue and event distribution pattern".[7] Short videos are highly interactive, immersive and emotionally resonant, which makes it rather simple to directly draw social attention in a specific scene and thus transform attention resources into content revenues.

Between 2015 and 2016, due to a general fall in TV turn-on rates, the decline of China's TV shopping industry was unavoidable. The growth rate of sales slowed down, entering a downward cycle. At that time, with Taobao as the pioneer, the livestreaming e-commerce model emerged, providing another possibility for the retail industry. In March 2016, Taobao Live was launched. Two years later, it received the home page recommendation of the Taobao application, and the number of daily active users quickly exceeded ten million. Due to the differences in resources such as channels, traffic, information and social relations for communication, as well as different traffic distribution mechanisms, the logic of livestreaming e-commerce based on short videos is not the same as that of e-commerce platforms like Taobao.

E-commerce platforms have an original gene of commodity trading, so it is more important to encourage high-quality content to obtain traffic and achieve traffic monetisation. Differently, short video platforms are featured with strong social interaction and connectivity, needing to link high-quality content to e-commerce consumption with the help of constant content mining. TikTok's traffic distribution is in line with the characteristics of a power law distribution, reflecting the obvious Matthew

[7] Xuhao Ran, "Distribution and Evaluation of Social Attention", *Social Sciences in Nanjing*, Vol. 4, 2010, pp. 47–53.

effect. In contrast, Kwai focuses more on traffic from undeveloped regions, reflecting a prominent "decentralisation" effect.

In 2017, the Kwai platform entered the field of livestreaming e-commerce and started a long-term layout. In 2018, TikTok conducted a large-scale e-commerce exploration through short videos and livestreams in various aspects, including business models and sales strategies, in order to cultivate its users' habit of consuming while watching the livestreams. Shortly after, in the first half of 2018, display windows on TikTok began to support links switching to Taobao, and users can also buy products through the platform's own online stores. At the same time, many influencers on Kwai opened "mini-shops", gathering traffic from their social circles to promote their own brands.

E-commerce based on social-networking platforms is essentially somewhat similar to that based on short video platforms in that both use content that is strongly entertaining or closely connected with life to attract fans, promote interaction, drive content-based consumption and repurchase. In November 2018, following Alibaba's investment in Red (Xiaohongshu), a popular Chinese social networking platform mainly targeted at young women, some content on Red was linked to specific products on Taobao. In the first quarter of 2019, Bilibili, one of China's largest online video platforms, began to cooperate with Alibaba in influencer marketing of e-commerce. In April 2019, some WeChat official accounts for the first time made explorations in livestreaming e-commerce. However, the rise of livestreaming e-commerce based on influencers has not yet caused fundamental changes to the competition landscape of e-commerce platforms. At present, the e-commerce models of TikTok, Kwai and Bilibili are still mainly focused on redirecting traffic to Taobao.

	Taobao Live	*Kwai*	*TikTok*	*WeChat*
Introduction of livestreaming e-commerce	2016	2018	2018	2019
Source of productions	Taobao/Tmall	Magic Chopsticks/Youzan/Taobao/Buy Together/Kwai	Taobao/Tmall	WeChat Mini Programmes
Estimate of DAU	Over 30 million	Over 100 million	Over 100 million	Unclear
Source of traffic	Taobao application (homepage)	Kwai Marketing (on-platform marketing service)	Information flow advertising on TikTok	WeChat Official Accounts
MCN participation	Very high	Hardly any	High	Average
Censorship	Very strict	Flexible	Strict	Strict
Hot category of products	Apparel/Beauty/Food/Jewellery	Low-margin products	Beauty	Unclear

With technical support, the consumption pattern based on short videos is more innovative. E-commerce not only helps short video platforms with content distribution, but also provides the audience with daily information. The demand for people to watch videos on mobile was booming in 2020 due to the pandemic, and the time spent on short videos has been longer than that spent on mobile games, hence the fierce competition for social attention resources among short video platforms such as TikTok and Kwai. The average number of daily active users and the daily usage time per capita of short video applications have increased significantly compared with 2019. According to Aurora Mobile, the number of daily active users of TikTok reached a peak of 311 million during the Spring Festival holiday in 2020, seeing a year-on-year rise of 93.1%. Meanwhile, Kwai ranked second with 177 million daily active users, an increase of 55.8% over the same period last year, while the number of daily active users of Watermelon (Xigua Videos) reached 45.8 million, increasing by 30% year-on-year.[8] In terms of livestream, Kwai now takes up more than half of the traffic of the entire market, owing much to its millions of core users who mostly resident in minor cities and rural regions.

In terms of operational mechanisms, firstly, short video platforms maintain efficient control over content distribution based on big data, algorithmic recommendations and the logic of traffic monetisation. For instance, the first video or livestream that a user sees every day when he/she opens TikTok is the result of precise computations by the platform with the help of artificial intelligence. Users' following lists, the number of videos clicked, trending lists of the platform and even usage behaviours like searching and browsing are all accurately recorded and become an important reference for the platform's content distribution. In addition, in order to control the attention of users, TikTok has added a "lock mode". Normally, it is a basic setting for short video applications to allow users to swipe their fingers up and down to switch between videos. In that way, users can simply swipe away any video or livestream they are not interested in, but recently some users have found that gesture does not work when watching certain livestreams and they must return to the homepage or close the application.

In the terms of platform regulation, short video platforms, typically represented by TikTok, keep controlling the quality of user-generated

[8] Yang Junfeng, "Short Video Facing New Challenges", *China Newspaper Industry*, Vol. 11, 2020, pp. 48–49.

content and improving the ecological environment of the whole industry. The rules for livestreaming e-commerce are constantly upgraded to avoid potential risks. On August 14, 2020, TikTok introduced the "Regulation on Product Dispatching", which clearly defines "overtime dispatch"; that is, merchants/hosts fail to dispatch products within the promised time and upload a valid logistics order number to the platform. Whenever a purchase order is identified as "overtime dispatch", it will be recorded by the platform. If the same product is dispatched out of time more than twice in total, it will be banned from sale. If no action is taken by the merchant/host despite multiple penalties, the platform reserves the right to close the shop as appropriate. Even a small fine of RMB 10 will be imposed for every ordinary violation of the rules. According to current regulations, the maximum deduction of shop deposit in a single day will not exceed RMB 500. Moreover, each time a merchant/host is found to have made a false dispatch, the platform will deduct 500 RMB from the deposit, with the maximum deduction in a single day not exceeding 5,000 RMB.

Besides, TikTok has also issued specific regulations on the release of videos with product links, segmenting livestream hosts based on traffic they obtained. For accounts with less than 1,000 followers, they can only release one video with product links every week, while accounts with 1,000 to 3,000 fans, accounts with 3,000 to 10,000 fans and accounts with 10,000 fans and above can respectively release 2, 5 and 10 videos with product links each day. This means that with the platform's emphasis on brand voice and IP value, the greater the hosts' traffic, the higher the quality of marketing resources they will obtain. It is consequent that their accounts, which benefit the most from the platform's traffic distribution rules based on account segmentation and traffic centralisation, are always of great value of traffic monetisation and thus superior in marketing performance. It is worth noting that short video platforms pay special attention to the regulation of KOL accounts in the field of beauty. By re-selecting cosmetic products, the platforms conduct strict quality control, sifting out high-quality products for future influencer marketing. Beauty products are highly concerned by TikTok in its commercialisation. Because of their outstanding performance in traffic monetisation and high commission rates, beauty and personal care products are very popular among influencers on TikTok, accounting for the majority of the products they sell.

3.3 Short Video Value Extension: Effective Marketing and E-Commerce Closed Loop

The evolution of the traffic-based economy to community-based economy has become inevitable. When traditional retail was dominant, the acquisition of traffic mainly depended on offline advertising. While in the era of mobile Internet, due to the emergence of digital scenes, there are more flexible and diverse ways to acquiring traffic, and the concept of community-based economy has been introduced, receiving considerable attention. Community-based marketing can effectively attract public traffic, the key to which is the creation of IPs with great market value.

Since 2018, apart from the entertainment function, other functions of TikTok, with the marketing function included, have also been gradually activated through transboundary integration. Many young users attracted by high-quality short videos are initially active on the platform with the identity of viewers or fans instead of consumers. They watch short videos, making comments and interacting with other users. In the context of the boom of we-media, these users are also able to make short videos themselves as creators. Unlike users of e-commerce applications such as Taobao, who are consumers from the very beginning, users of short video applications at first just use apps for entertainment purposes.

In China, the short video marketing strategy includes a general marketing rule known as the "golden seconds", which means short videos should quickly capture users' attention in three seconds, stimulating their purchase impulse and shortening the time it takes to make decisions. TikTok has innovatively launched a shopping cart function, which supports links switching to e-commerce platforms, thus forming a complete e-commerce chain based on short videos, which helps brands to quickly realise traffic monetisation. Beauty and personal care products contribute a major part of the revenues generated from short video marketing based on TikTok.

Another highlight of short video marketing is the combination of UGC and KOLs. The proportion of user-generated content in the overall content of short video platforms is greater than that of KOL marketing content, which reflects the initiative of users and that they regard TikTok as a platform for self-presentation. Based on specific content templates offered by the platform, users can take imitation videos, adding their own creativity. Attractive content will bring likes and followers to the creators, meanwhile gaining more traffic resources from the platform. As a result, circle-breaking social interaction has become the key to short video marketing success. Because of the traffic bonus, TikTok has attracted numerous promising new brands.

The celebrity effect is also an essential part of the short video marketing strategy. By inviting celebrities, especially highly influential actors, to endorse their products, brands may reach more prospective consumers and further realise traffic monetisation.

From brands setting up official accounts and conducting short video marketing, what short video platforms intend to form is a closed loop of e-commerce self-sufficiency, though at present even TikTok and Kwai must reluctantly rely on shopping links that direct users to third-party e-commerce applications due to the incompletion of a self-built supply chain. This is the "two-step shopping procedure" we are to discuss later. Also, it is worth noting that users' consumption habits are also being gradually changed by short video platforms, transforming from passive reception to active search and purchase. For its users, TikTok is no longer just an entertainment application. For brands, they can transform public traffic of the platform into their own private traffic through short video marketing, in order to receive maximum revenues.

CHAPTER 2

Market Overview for Livestreaming E-Commerce

Abstract This chapter gives a comprehensive introduction to the technical and social environment of livestreaming e-commerce as well as government policies and regulations concerning the industry. Based on the 5G infrastructure, advanced technologies such as UHD, 3D audio, VR and AR will provide an immersive experience for users watching livestreaming. Also, people's home isolation during the pandemic in 2020 promotes the prosperity of online entertainment and consumption industries. Livestreaming e-commerce develops rapidly. At the end of this chapter, the author gives an overview of China's livestreaming e-commerce market. According to official data, not only the industry grows fast, but the profitability of livestreaming e-commerce has also been verified in practice.

Keywords Technical infrastructure · Social environment · Government policies · Market potential

1 Technical Environment

The issuance of 5G commercial licenses has given rise to the rapid implementation of 5G applications. Compared with 4G, 5G, which is characterised by high speed and low delay, has achieved notable improvement

R. Si, *China Livestreaming E-commerce Industry Insights*, https://doi.org/10.1007/978-981-16-5344-5_2

in key performance parameters. This will bring revolutionary changes to the production and transmission of audio-visual content, contributing to the creation of more attractive and interactive videos.

Based on the 5G infrastructure, advanced technologies such as UHD, 3D audio, VR and AR will provide an immersive experience for users watching livestreaming. With high-speed and stable 5G networks, the production and processing of VR content can be completed in the cloud within a short period of time, and the frame rate of videos can also be increased significantly. Therefore, the past business pain points of VR livestreams are solved. Users will have access to livestreaming panoramic scenes from the "first person perspective", maybe sooner than we imagine.

Overall, the application of new technologies has led to profound changes in all aspects of livestreaming e-commerce. Livestream rooms have become important online consumption venues for society members to interact and share information. Meanwhile, livestreams have been introduced into tourism, physical retail and other industries, with different types of livestreams providing users with a variety of consumption options. During the COVID-19 pandemic in 2020, for instance, online tourist livestreams motivated consumers' impulsive consumption behaviour and maximised the long tail effect. TikTok even launched a campaign called "Tourism Bureau in the Cloud", enabling users to enjoy the sceneries of popular tourist attractions without leaving home.

In addition, the mobile UI design of commercial livestreams enables a wider range of potential consumers to be reached, and mobile payment technology makes more secure and convenient transactions possible. At the same time, big data and cloud computing technology have realised multi-terminal synchronisation of consumer data, including product browsing records and purchase orders, as well as accurate real-time tracking of logistics.

2 Social Environment

Under the background of COVID-19 pandemic, the "lipstick effect" is rather evident; that is, the short-term economic downturn makes consumers more cautious about their purchases, and as a result, sales of expensive products fall sharply while that of cheap goods increase significantly. People's home isolation due to lockdown policies promotes the prosperity of online entertainment and consumption industries. Livestreaming e-commerce develops rapidly (Graphs 1 and 2).

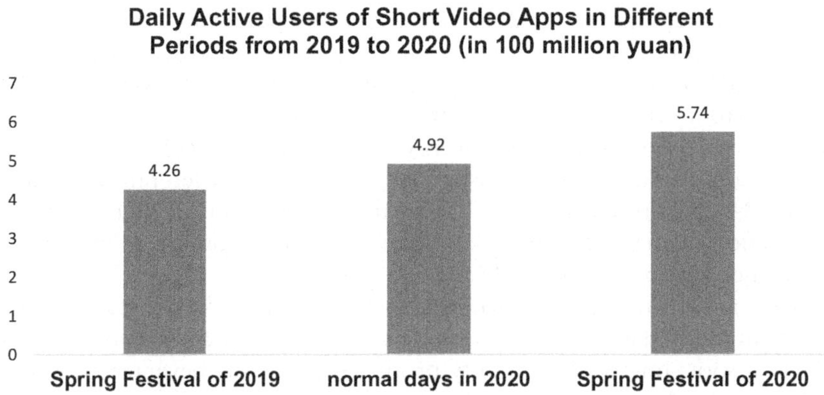

Graph 1 This chart mainly illustrates daily active users of Chinese short video apps in different periods from 2019 to 2020 (in 100 million yuan), especially during the Spring Festival compared to the normal days

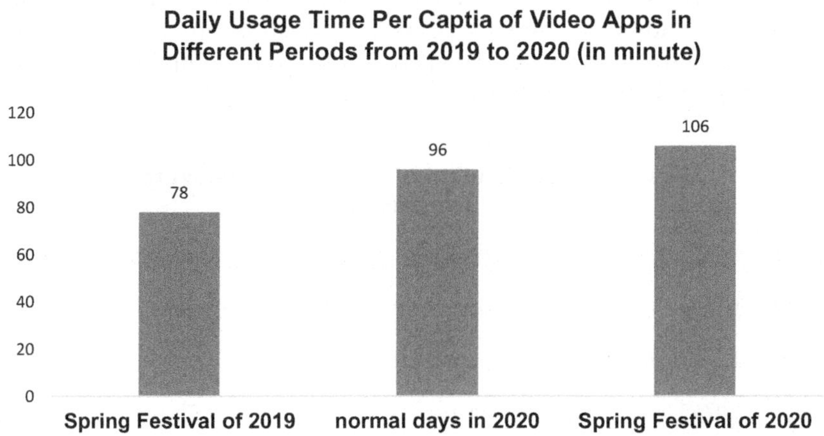

Graph 2 This chart mainly illustrates daily usage time per capita of Short Video Apps in Different Periods from 2019 to 2020 (in minute), especially during the Spring Festival compared to the normal days

The average number of daily active users and the daily usage time per capita of short video applications in 2020 both increased significantly compared to 2019. In terms of livestream e-commerce, Kwai in 2020 took up more than half of the traffic of the entire market. As for the age structure of users, livestream viewers of Kwai were mainly 25–35 years old while those of TikTok were mostly 24–30 years old. Differently, teenagers under 24 constituted the main livestream viewer group of Bilibili. The Z generation, namely users born later than 1995, is becoming an important consumer group (Graphs 3, 4, and 5).

Generally, during the pandemic, traffic on TikTok was mainly distributed to daily necessities, with clothing products keeping taking the top spot, followed by beauty products, food and beverage products (Graphs 6 and 7).

In terms of participating enterprises, the number of enterprises adopting livestreaming e-commerce has continued to climb since 2019 when the industry saw an explosive growth. In that year, the growth rate of business registrations rose to 91.82% from 53.78% in 2018. According to the State Administration for Market Regulation, in the first half of 2020, over 9,000 livestream-related enterprises were set up in China, with a year-on-year increase of 409%.

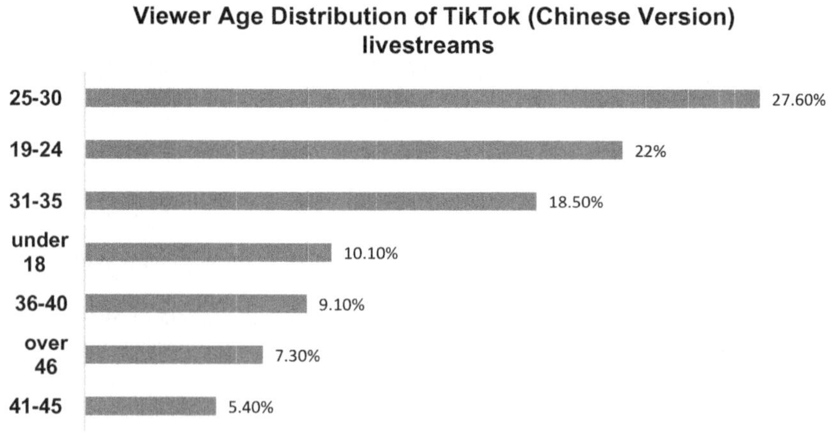

Graph 3 This chart mainly illustrates viewer age distribution of TikTok (Chinese version) livestreams

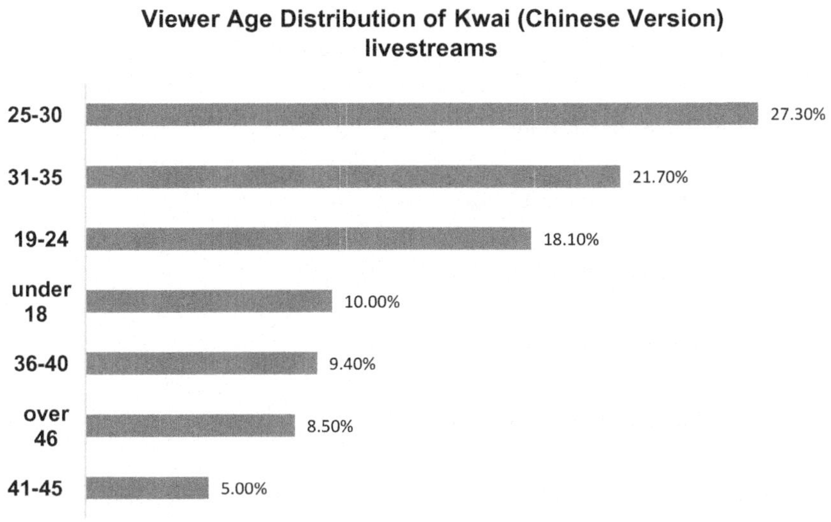

Graph 4 This chart mainly illustrates viewer age distribution of Kwai (Chinese version) livestreams

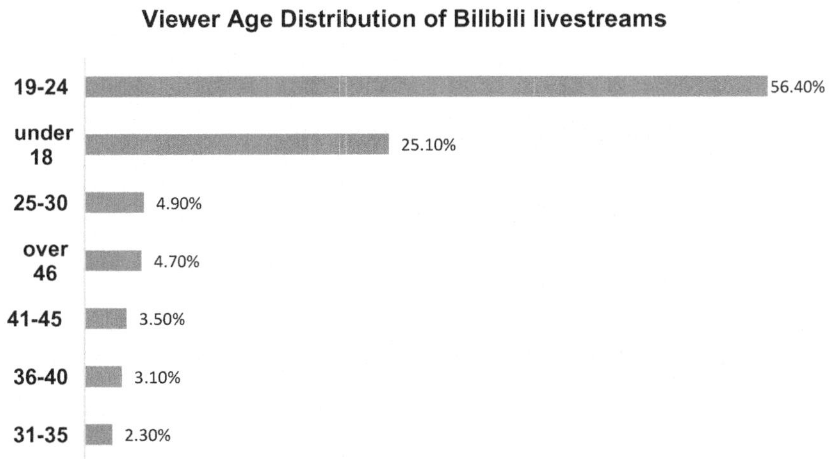

Graph 5 This chart mainly illustrates viewer age distribution of Bilibili (Chinese version) livestreams

Graph 6 This chart mainly illustrates recommendation Traffic Distribution of TikTok (Chinese Version) in different categories

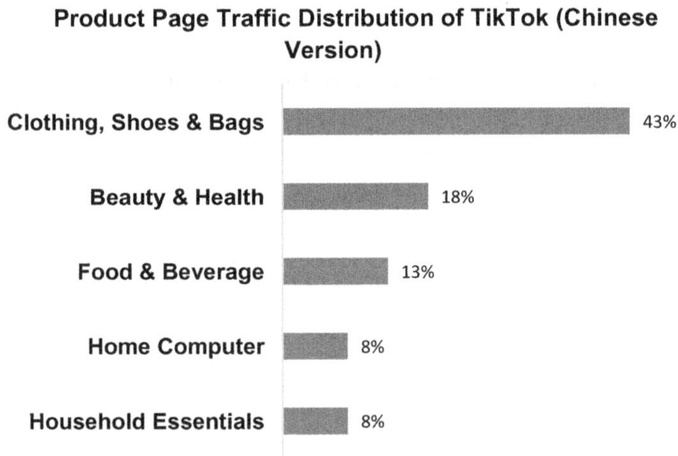

Graph 7 This chart mainly illustrates Product Page Traffic Distribution of TikTok (Chinese Version) in different categories

At present, there are nearly 18,000 registered enterprises in operation, which include the word "livestream" in their name, business scope or brand name. These enterprises have a concentrated geographical distribution, mostly located in southern cities. In Hangzhou, Zhejiang Province, known as the "city of livestreams", there are more than 2,300 livestream-related enterprises, accounting for 13.12% of the national total, and Hangzhou is also home to the company of Viya, who has the title of "top host" on Taobao Live. During economic transformation, e-commerce has also become a key area of economic development for northern cities. Liaoning Province, located in the north, has issued a series of policies to support livestreaming e-commerce in recent years, making the number of livestream-related enterprises in Liaoning Province second only to Hangzhou, reaching more than 1700.

The boundaries of industries involved in livestreaming e-commerce are still expanding, from daily necessities to beauty products and empowering services such as political communication and poverty alleviation. In terms of industry distribution, 35.04% of livestream-related enterprises in China are in the business services sector, 23.53% in the culture, sports and entertainment sectors, 22.23% in the software and IT services sector.

3 Government Policies and Regulations

3.1 Livestreaming E-Commerce: A New Engine for Urban Development

In China's livestreaming e-commerce, the government policy participation is not only reflected in the diversiform support that promotes the independent development of the industry, but also in each practitioner's compliance with the standardised guidelines issued by relevant departments. From the government's perspective only have the supervision departments led the industry to a marketing environment that is capable of self-discipline will the industry yield positive social value. Therefore, multi-dimensional supports and standardised guidance from the superior authority have been going concurrently.

The government intervene has shaped the newly formed industry not only an economic growth point, but a new vessel for China's urban development also. The plan is to use urban areas as a series of original points and commercial livestreams as engines, having the economy-stimulating power radiate out and integrating economic resources. According to relevant statistics, 11 cities across China have successively made reginal policies regarding livestreaming e-commerce, in accordance with the local environments, while feasible plans and strategies for the development of the industry in certain areas have been introduced to increase the regional influence. At present, southern cities of China such as Shanghai, Guangzhou and Hangzhou are pioneering the ambitious strategy.

The strategic goal of Guangzhou, which is to make the city a national livestreaming e-commerce capital, is rather evident. On March 23, 2020 Guangzhou Municipal Commerce Bureau issued the "Notice on Printing and Distributing Guangzhou Livestreaming E-Commerce Development Plan (2020–2022)", from the perspectives of top-level design, industrial clusters, e-commerce entities, etc., to use livestreaming e-commerce to catalyse the real economy, namely "Project One-Ten-Hundred-Thousand", through 12 elaborately formulated policies and a plan to train 10,000 livestream experts.

On May 15, 2020, Shanghai MCN Professional Committee was established, which is the first professional committee in China regarding influencer marketing and content production. Shanghai, as one of the most economically prosperous cities in China, by then was already qualified for a full development of influencer economy, with abundant resources such as that of space, finance, storage and delivery to rely on, which was why it was chosen as a business stronghold for long-term careers by the leading practitioners in the expertise like Li Jiaqi, who is called by his fans the "top boy of livestreaming e-commerce". Their later successes have also proved that Shanghai has huge potential and an e-commerce environment that are attractive to the practitioners and sustainable enough to retain them. Therefore, the industry's development in Shanghai aims specifically at the cultivation of a domestic gathering of "influencer economy", to promote the upstream and downstream exchanges of the industry's value chain nationwide.

Different from Guangzhou and Shanghai, Hangzhou is committed to building a national livestreaming e-commerce central base as a model example in the industry. To boost the livestreaming e-commerce and influencer economy as well as to empower traditional enterprises, Hangzhou has established the "Hangzhou Future Science and Technology E-commerce Enterprise Alliance" and made a development plan called "Livestream-Traditional Economy Bidirectional Interaction" which matched the top-level design and policies. In addition, the Department of Commerce of Zhejiang and Alibaba Group jointly initiated the "Village

Livestreaming Plan", which led to a dramatic promotion of e-commerce in the rural areas, as in the "Livestreaming Season of Zhejiang's Better Life", with Viya appointed as the representative and an inspiriting slogan for farmers: "Make everyone livestream host, make every phone your farm tool, make livestreams your farm work, and make Internet data your production and harvest". By exploring and introducing new marketing models, the Zhejiang government is in the hope of accelerating the development of rural e-commerce and the overall economy alike.

As for northern China, Yingkou, a coastal city in Liaoning Province, has issued the "Yingkou Livestreaming E-Commerce Development Plan (2020–2022)", which includes a local-oriented marketing model called "livestreaming e-commerce + models". The new model was created to promote transboundary empowerment through several e-commerce-based cross-industry combinations, such as "livestreaming e-commerce + local industries", "livestreaming e-commerce + precise poverty alleviation", "livestreaming e-commerce + county economy", "livestreaming e-commerce + business districts", "livestreaming e-commerce + border-crossing", "livestreaming e-commerce + exhibitions", "livestreaming e-commerce + Customer-to-Manufacturer" and "livestreaming e-commerce + craftsmanship". Through elaborately tailored strategy, the Yingkou government expects to decorate itself with livestream business districts featured with local characteristics, as well as to further blend livestreaming e-commerce with the city's supply chain.

3.2 Segmentation and Standardisation of Government Regulations

As soon as they got involved in livestreaming e-commerce, the public authorities decided to settle some controversial matters tangling in the industry, such as suspicious statistics, inappropriate content, questionable product quality and some hosts' fragile public credibility, which were defined as "chaos". Though the definition of "chaos" was somehow without specification, many of the controversial matters regarded by the definition seemed to be too chaotic for a legal market indeed. Resolved to eradicate all sorts of violations that kept the industry from "self-discipline", relevant government departments stressed the livestreaming platforms with a series of laws and regulations, showing the "chaos" zero tolerance. As response to the enforcement, the platforms fell in line and made attempts to standardise their supply chain management and after-sales services, as well as to strengthen risk control by focusing more on user complaints, content-based marketing and qualification assessment. In March 2016, more than 20 Internet platforms including Baidu, Sina, Sohu and iQiyi jointly issued the "Beijing Livestreaming Industry Self-Discipline Convention", which stipulates that livestreams on every relevant platform must be watermarked and that livestream content without exception ought to be kept for no less than 15 days for prospective regulation. Since then, the platforms started strict qualification assessment on users participating in livestreaming e-commerce, and those who generated content related to politics, guns, drugs, violence and pornography were to be blacklisted, while the real-time supervision was prolonged to 24 hours a day. Two months later, the National Radio and Television Administration issued the "Notice on the Enhancement of Online Livestreaming Audiovisual Programme Service Management", in which the details of supervision are listed more specifically and clearly, covering every dimension of livestreaming e-commerce from participants such as hosts, guests and audience to everything released or to be released, no matter it is livestream content generated by hosts or real-time floating comments from fans.

In November 2016, based on a series of foregoing government documents including the "Decision of the Standing Committee of the National People's Congress on Strengthening the Security of Internet Information", the "Notice of State Department on Authorising Cyberspace Administration to Implement Management of Internet Information Service", the "Internet Information Service Management Measures" and the "Internet News Information Service Management Regulation", the Cyberspace Administration issued the "Internet Livestream services Management Regulation" to thoroughly guide the industry to a morally decent environment, as well as to further regulate livestream practitioners' behaviours online. It has everything in common with the previously released specifications regarding hosts and platforms, stating that only hosts and platforms regarded as qualified are allowed to continue Internet news information service, only with more concrete descriptions of platform's obligations, such as to construct a complete, systematic network for content supervision, to deploy professionals commensurate with the scale of livestream services and to improve information censorship, data security, duty inspection, emergency response and technical support. It also stipulates that for every livestream involving Internet news broadcasting service, an editor-in-chief must be appointed and responsible, and such content must be censored before release. At the same time, the Cyberspace Administration also urged relevant departments to pay special attention to the frequent occurrence of indecent and vulgar content on livestream platforms that were deemed as pollution to the Internet environment. Furthermore, it proposed to implement hierarchical management on hosts according to the number of fans and the nature of content. Lastly, the administration decrees that livestream activities of illegal nature, including those that are considered as potential to endanger national security, disrupt social stability, infringe on the legal rights and interests of others, spread obscene and pornographic content, are all strictly forbidden.

On December 2, 2016, the Ministry of Culture released the "Administrative Measures for Cyberspace Performing and Marketing Activities" and defied "cyberspace performing activities" as performance-driven cultural products that are produced and disseminated in real time, or uploaded in the form of recorded audios and videos, through the Internet, mobile communication network, mobile Internet and other information networks. Like the previous documents, this one also urges the platforms to tighten the real-time self-censorship of livestream content, aiming to establish a content regulating mechanism and allocate specialised censors and technical supervisors in place. From then on, online performers are demanded to register and verify their real names, and platforms are required to improve their user registration systems, with the purpose of protecting users' personal information as well as supervising their expressions and activities in the livestream cyberspace. In short, the ministry intends to build through the regulation a stable public credibility, a far-reaching binding power and the industry's strong awareness of self-supervision.

In June 2017, the Central Internet Information Office conducted an inspection on 50 major corporations specialising in cyberspace performance. More than 30 livestream platforms including YY Live, Dragon Ball Live (Longzhu Live), Huomao Live and Miaopai were investigated and punished. Some highly popular platforms, such as Volcano and Huajiao, were also found guilty for spreading rumours and false information that were considered as disruptions of social order. In the inspection, a total of 10 online performance platforms were shut down, 48 corporations accepted administrative punishment, 30,235 livestream rooms were closed and 3,382 were rectified; meanwhile, 31,371 performers were penalised and 547 performance contracts were forced to be terminated.[1]

In August 2018, the National Radio and Television Administration, the National Internet Information Office and other six departments jointly issued the "Notice on Strengthening the Management of Internet Livestream services" to intensify licensing and filing management of livestream services providers. In terms of content supervision, information filtering and user complaints, the notice seeks to establish and optimise the management mechanism and apply technical control to impede illegal activities on the livestream platforms. Other than that, it also provides clear guidance on hosts' dress code, basic qualification, content production and that on the establishment of direct report/complaint channels that are functional 24 hours a day for immediate user management. To any report and complaint, platforms are ordered to respond within no longer than 90 seconds.

In February 2019, Tencent Video released the "Announcement on Standardisation of Livestream Behaviours", whose livestream platform was then known for the prosperity of video game livestreams with numerous active users. Sine video game livestreams are strongly interactive with abundant and widely-scattered audience; Tencent considered it as a risk control to specify the standards of livestream behaviours regarding video games. The company emphasises in the announcement on their copyright protecting mechanism and marketing regulation concerning authorised content, which are both standardised as the announcement reads: "A video game is naturally related in copyrights to any livestream using it as content. As a content provider in the livestreaming industry and its derivative fields, Tencent bears the responsibility of ensuring every authorised video game's compliance with relevant laws and regulations, and the duty of promoting the standardisation of livestream content".

In addition to that, Tencent's livestream management also issued a letter titled "A Letter to Business Partners and Practitioners Using Our Livestream services", expecting to build a connection between content and platform service so that they may cultivate a high-quality user group possible to create greater commercial value and new possibilities for

[1] "CCTV Exposes the Live Broadcasting Platform Chaos and the Live Broadcast Industry Will Start Strong Supervision", released by China Business Network on April 3, 2018. http://www.chinairn.com/news/20180403/142305883.shtml.

the company to explore in public relations. On July 20, 2020, the Tencent Video platform opened a free entry to attract more individuals and enterprises to participate in their livestream business. There were no more threshold for users to host a livestream, and the rules for livestreaming e-commerce were also adjusted. Meanwhile, the platform announced six privileges for its enterprise users, whom were also known as "Blue Vs" for the symbol that marked their accounts. From then on, the Blue V users have had the convenience of conducting commercial livestreams with a mini programme offered by the platform and activated for them automatically, which brings audience from Kandian Live, one of Tencent's subsidiary video platforms, one way straight to the privileged users' own mini programmes where their products are in display. Tencent also addressed at this point their plans to provide traffic support customised for the Blue Vs, which would allow them to participate in the online events officially organised by Tencent Live, enjoy exclusive customer service and have the earliest try on any digital products released on Tencent Live. Aside from that, in order to facilitate the users' understanding of this policy upgrade, Tencent Live put online a tutorial called "Tencent Livestream Classroom", which provided all users with free introductions to the platform's digital productions, e-commerce knowledge, and tricks and skills to get the hang of the new marketing model. And almost simultaneously, Baidu, as a trendsetter of the Chinese Internet other than Tencent, had completed the construction of their own livestream platform, the assembling of the operation team and the assignment of the chief executive in charge of the livestream section, in the efforts of the company's mobile-ecomanagement group. To a thorough mining of the newly-rising market the giant was on its way, with the Internet-based thinking it recognised as no stranger.

3.3 Merchants, Hosts, Platforms, Users: Definitions, Rights and Obligations

Since 2020, the livestream industry has been booming and yielded noteworthy value as a highly socialised marketing model, which led to a surge of purchasing power in the Chinese market. However, as multiple platforms are eager to share a piece of the prosperity, there is no lack of good signs as well as worrying one. The contradictory situation has led to the first regulatory document that intervenes the marketing matters of the industry, namely the "Regulation of Online Livestream Marketing Activities" released by China Advertising Association on June 24, 2020, and officially implemented a week later on July 1, as a forerunning guidance on the shaping of the industrial ecology and the balance between market evolution and intervention of standardisation. However, since the regulation was initiated by China Advertising Association, it by nature does not have compulsory legal effect on every participant in the industry, but on the members of the association only.

Be that as it may, the regulation still gives to the industry a concise definition of each kind of participants with a clear classification, followed by descriptions of their responsibilities and obligations. In the regulation, livestream merchants are defined as individuals or corporations who supply products or provide services in livestream marketing, and livestream hosts are referred to individuals who directly interact with users of the platforms in livestream marketing activities, while livestreaming platforms are described as all kinds of cyberspace that provides technical service and support for merchants and hosts, including platforms focusing on e-commerce, audio-visual content and social networking. And livestream agency is the title for individuals and organisations specialising in training hosts, cultivating talents and offering marketing support for those who wish to preside over their own livestreams. And users, of course, are referred to organisations and individuals that make purchases of commodities or services in the livestream cyberspace.

Furthermore, the Regulation states the basic principles that every participant in the industry shall follow. In the general respect, it demands the participants to adhere to every previous government-issued regulation, as well as to act by the code of honest and fair competition. In terms of product quality, it states that product introduction that is inaccurate and exaggerated is strictly forbidden, as all participants are fully responsible for their own product selection and quality control. In terms of livestreaming data, it stresses that the data environment must be purified of purchase order fakery and credibility speculation to avoid Internet traffic bubbles and any credibility evaluation system that is fraudulent and misleading. In terms of information protection, it reminds the platforms of protecting consumer's personal information from leaking in due course, and that collecting and using user's personal information shall abide by laws, administrative regulations and other relevant provisions, and intellectual property protection mechanisms should be established.

Also, the regulation lists the qualifications that are needed, the varieties of commodities and services that are allowed, and the right and obligation relationship among participants that is to be aware of for one to participate in the livestream industry. When a merchant enters a livestream platform, for instance, genuine information of personal or corporation identity, contact details, business license and relevant certificates must be checked by the platform. As for products or services to be promoted, product quality, product safety in use and service's nature and content shall be comply with the standards established in relevant laws and regulations. Explicitly formulated as they were, most of the provisions in the Regulation are the general codes to live by in an ordinary market environment, rather than obligations particularly binding on the participants in the livestream industry. Even some of the controversial provisions, the requirement of real-name registration, for one, has been accepted by many as a necessity to protect consumer's right, facilitate platform's supervision and guarantee better after-sales service.

4 Overview of China's Livestreaming E-Commerce Market

It can be tracked back to 2017 when commercial livestreams first emerged on the Chinese Internet. Then, in the following three years, the newly-rising industry's market size increased from 20 billion RMB to 433.8 billion RMB. According to the statistics from iiMedia Research, the number of livestream users in China reached 617 million in 2020, which increased by 184 million compared with the first half of 2019, as most livestream users were concentrated in the fields of video game and e-commerce, who had boosted the market sizes of China's livestreaming e-commerce and video game livestreams respectively to 961 billion RMB and 30.03 billion RMB in the same year (Graph 8).

China's livestream market by then had shown four prominent features, which continued to exist till the present day. The first feature is that the high density of audience has been "sinking" geographically, which means the first- and second-tier cities have been losing livestream audience gradually, and meanwhile, the third- and fourth-tier cities, as well as small towns and villages, keep gaining advantage in this respect. Currently, the less developed regions own livestreaming audience that are superior both in numbers and loyalty.

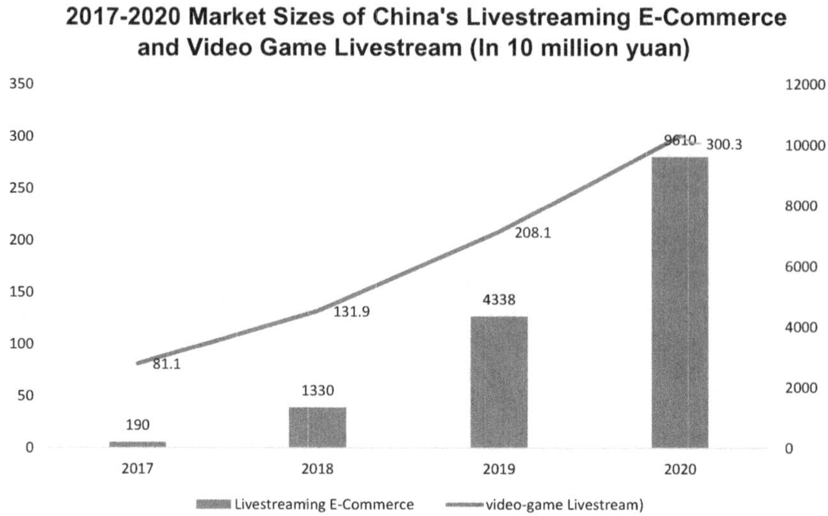

Graph 8 This chart mainly illustrates The overall Market Sizes of China's Livestreaming E-Commerce and Video Game Livestream from 2017 to 2020 (in 10 million yuan)

The second feature shows the livestreaming content is growing more and more complex and disorderly, while user's attention is captured mostly by content of pan-entertainment.

Thirdly, the hosts have become ever more specialised, while the proportions of the leading hosts, the average ones and those lagging behind are rather unbalanced.

And lastly, in terms of monetisation methods, the industry has made breakthroughs from traditional methods, such as advertisement monetisation, and developed several transboundary methods including "celebrity + livestreaming show" and "e-sports + PGC", which hatched more possibilities for monetisation.

In the entire e-commerce market, high-quality traffic entries (like homepages of Taobao applications) stay on the highest level of brand concentration and are also strategic points the merchants contest for. Traditional e-commerce corporations such as Taobao have solved the problem of product variety insufficiency in the traditional retail industry, while visuo-spatial e-commerce platforms such as TikTok and Kwai can easily incite users' willingness and arouse inactive users' desire to purchase. The traditional and new platforms complement as well as leverage each other.

Taobao's livestream services started earlier and has a high level of verticalisation. It has accumulated a stable amount of traffic in virtue of millions of loyal users, whose dependence on the Taobao platform has been well fostered in the last few years. As one of the many results, Taobao succeeded in covering the whole industry with its steadily expanding influence and now has entered a period of rapid development. From 2017 to 2019, the Taobao platform's online merchandise volume in the field of livestreaming e-commerce doubled and hit a new peak in 2019. During the Double Eleven shopping day of 2019, commercial livestreams on the Taobao platform generated nearly 20 billion RMB in turnover, while the company's total livestreaming e-commerce turnover reached 250 billion RMB this year. According to Alibaba's financial report of the fourth quarter of 2020, the GMV generated from Taobao's commercial livestreams exceeded 400 billion RMB, and the annual GMV of 177 hosts reached 100 million RMB. In the same year, of the 500 billion RMB generated from TikTok's e-commerce, only 20% was contributed by TikTok's own online stores, and rest was created by purchase orders on third-party platforms. Now, TikTok plans to raise the GMV target of 2021 to 1,000 billion RMB, which will double the volume of the previous year if it succeeds. As for Kwai, one of TikTok's strongest competitors, there were in total more than 1.4 billion livestreaming activities on Kwai applications in 2020, and the company's e-commerce GMV grew to 204.1 billion RMB, with an average repurchase rate of over 65%, according to the "2020 Annual Content Report" released by Kwai's big data research team.

It is almost a foregone conclusion that with more companies joining the game in the post-epidemic period, the competition among various platforms will grow even more intense than it is at present. Such being the case, it will be more crucial for a platform to position itself precisely in the big picture. To this, those content-based, rather than e-commerce-oriented platforms such as TikTok ought to be more attentive.

According to the 47th "Statistics Report on Status of China's Internet Development" released by CNNIC (China Internet Network Information Center), as of December 2020, the number of Internet users in China was 989 million, and the Internet penetration rate reached 70.4%, while China's online retail sales increased by 10.9% compared with 2019 and reached 11.76 trillion RMB, in which the retail sales of physical goods are 9.76 trillion RMB, accounting for 24.9% of the total domestic retail sales of consumer goods. The number of online shopping users rose by 72.15 million compared with March 2020 and reached 782 million, accounting for 79.1% of the total number of Chinese netizens. Livestreaming e-commerce also saw a growth of popularity that, according to the report, the new shopping model had become so welcome that 66.2% of livestreaming e-commerce users had made at least one purchase when watching commercial livestreams. The improvement also opened new prospects for the government, for when it comes to foreign trades, livestreaming e-commerce may as well yield remarkable value if it complies with the "double-circulation" strategy implemented domestically and globally alike, and meanwhile gives full play to its cross-border trade-facilitating potential.

Another case is that online payment has become more popular and common since the rise of livestreaming e-commerce. As of December 2020, the number of online payment users in China has reached 854 million. Integrated with supply chains, online payment now can be of great assistance to livestream merchants in providing precise market information. As for most consumers, online payment is no more some cutting-edge Internet technology that deserves their vigilance, judging by the steady growth of its user base and utilisation rate that has laid the very foundation of the livestream industry's large-scale expansion.

According to Alibaba's big data research group, video game livestream users make up the largest proportion of livestream audience in China. As of 2020, there were about 260 million active users in the video game livestreaming cyberspace, more than frequenters of reality show livestreams, concert livestreams and sport livestreams that grew to 207 million, 150 million and 213 million, respectively, in the same year. Apparently, the geographically "sinking" high density of audience played an important part in the growth of the market, since many newcomers were from less developed cities and rural regions (Graphs 9).

Furthermore, Alibaba's research group divides livestream users by age into three groups, namely Generation X (born between 1965 and 1980), Generation Y (born between 1980 and 1995) and the Generation Z (born later than 1995). The result shows that the first group prefers products they are familiar with, the second group is more attracted by famous brands, and the third group displays a strong loyalty to celebrities. As

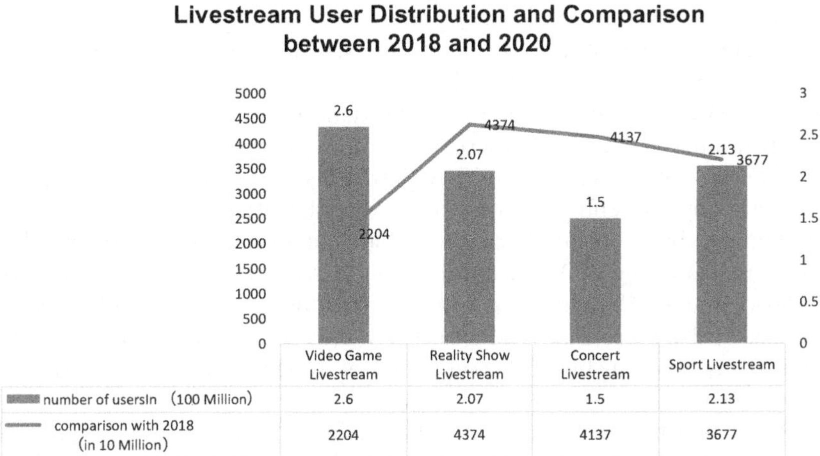

Graph 9 This chart mainly illustrates The overall Market Sizes of China's Livestreaming E-Commerce and Video Game Livestream from 2017 to 2020 (in 10 million yuan)

for the junior citizens in the third group who were born after the millennium, they choose to put more trust in the Internet influencers than in the traditional celebrities such as film and television stars. In the result, we can clearly see the progressive changes of consumer demands and trust orientation over the past 50 years.

As Internet traffic now is concentrated in the short video cyberspace, the rapid growth of short video users has also been a driving force behind the development of the livestream industry. As of December 2020, the number of online video users in China reached 927 million, including 873 million short video users, which increased by 100 million compared with March 2020, accounting for 88.3% of netizens. The proportion of content-oriented videos also went up significantly; meanwhile, there were more content revealing uploader's personal intention and providing digital experience that focused more on the sense of immersion, illimitation and scene-orientation. The large number of Internet users has sustained the prosperity of China's consumer market and founded a stable user base for the digital economy. It is as well a key power source that energises online services and consumption, making them new impetuses for the growth of the economy, especially in the time of the epidemic when the consumption-driving power of livestreaming e-commerce is fully released. So, it is not surprising that the market fuelled by the livestream industry has exploded, bathing in consumer's attention.

The Ministry of Commerce's big data monitoring shows that in the first quarter of 2020, there were more than 4 million commercial livestreams conducted on multiple platforms, along with an average of 30,000 people opening online stores every day after the outbreak of the epidemic, while the number of merchants stationed on livestream platforms increased by 700%. According to the statistics recently disclosed by Taobao, the GMV generated from livestreams on the Taobao platform has grown by more than 150% for three consecutive years. Not only the industry grows fast, but the profitability of livestreaming e-commerce has also been verified in practice.

According to the report titled "Professional Talents in the Livestream Industry" and released by Zhaopin and Taobao List in the spring of 2020, the number of new livestream merchants on Taobao Live in February 2020 rose by 719%; the demand for livestream talents increased by 132% year-on-year; and the per capita monthly salary in the platform's livestream profession was 9,845 RMB. The report also indicates that the platform had presented over 1.4 million livestreams related to agricultural products, covering 31 provinces and over 2,000 counties across the country, and more than 60,000 farmers joined the business during the process. Based on the data from the report named "Current Situation of Practitioners of Livestreaming E-Commerce" provided by BOSS, a leading job-hunting website in China, that in the first three quarters of 2019, the per capita monthly salary of those who specialised in livestreaming e-commerce was 10,570 RMB nationwide and 12,160 RMB in Shanghai, with the latter being the highest in the country. The data also shows that Guangzhou and Hangzhou during that time were the two cities with the strongest demand for employees with livestreaming expertise. The shortage of skilled labour indicates that the industrial structure has become rather colossal and complex, and it is asking from the platforms for an upgrade in every dimension as well as a multi-dimensional breakthrough rather than mere balance maintaining. In terms of the industrial supply chain, for instance, since livestreaming e-commerce applies pulse-type marketing, a product will instantly become inventory if it cannot be sold in a month. And whenever a product's popularity is predicable, the supply chain ought to be adjusted accordingly as soon as practicable.

CHAPTER 3

Methodology of Influencer Marketing in Livestreaming E-Commerce

Abstract This chapter analyses influencers' marketing methodology in e-commerce livestreaming. Nowadays, the decline of celebrity-centred marketing has been unavoidable and the Matthew effect becomes evident, with some phenomenal hosts like Zhang Dayi, Li Jiaqi, Viya and Xin Ba dominating the market. Aside from Internet influencers and traditional celebrities, there are a great many corporate leaders who have adapted the changed marketing environment of e-commerce and made themselves part-time livestream hosts. This chapter also analyses host-audience interactions, which include preheating before livestreaming, host's self-empowerment and interactive entertainment. Creating hit products needs not only acquaintance-based promotion, but also the balance between high quality and low price. In livestreaming e-commerce, the sense of immersion is an important factor to be considered.

Keywords Marketing methodology · Internet influencers · Host-audience interactions · Sense of immersion

R. Si, *China Livestreaming E-commerce Industry Insights*, https://doi.org/10.1007/978-981-16-5344-5_3

1 The Phenomenal Hosts

1.1 *The Decline of Celebrity-Centred Marketing Coupled with the Matthew Effect*

It is rather conspicuous recently that the long-lasting heat of celebrity-centred marketing in China's livestream industry is cooling off, gradually surrendering to the new fashion that anyone can be a livestream host and sell goods online, despite the unevenness of traffic distribution and brand resources the minor hosts have to endure. The entering barriers of the livestream industry have been partly removed, hence the attraction to many newcomers of different social strata eager to test the waters. Data shows the number of Internet selling and marketing practitioners in China has already exceeded 10 million, and this number will continue to grow at a monthly rate of 8.8%. Livestreaming e-commerce now is not only limited to influencers supported by MCN organisations, but also includes mainstream media hosts, government officials, corporate CEOs, celebrities, retail shop owners and young people living in small cities or having special skills, even vocaloid stars such as Hatsune Miku. Compared to those who host professional TV home shopping programmes, common people who sell goods online appear to be more realistic and easier to resonant in emotion with the general population,[1] though their works often scent of deliberate performance. As KOLs, celebrities, artists, brand owners, government officials, traditional media practitioners and vocaloids all stepped into the livestream industry, the newly formed host class becomes increasingly diversified.

On the other hand, the leading hosts in the industry now attract more traffic and are more competent to sell merchandise than ever before, which once more demonstrates the Matthew effect. According to the report titled "Livestreaming E-Commerce Moving Toward a Trillion Billion Market" jointly released by Alibaba's research group and KPMG, 2% of the e-commerce hosts have harvested nearly 80% of the GMV market share. During the Double Eleven shopping festival in 2020, the revenues that Viya and Li Jiaqi made on Taobao reached 12.3 billion RMB and 9.8 billion RMB, respectively; Xin Ba, a top host on the Kwai

[1] Peng Lan, "Connecting and Anti-Connecting: Swaying Rules of the Internet", *Chinese Journal of Journalism & Communication*, Vol. 2, 2019.

platform, sold products that valued 2.8 billion RMB; the sales performance of Luo Yonghao, a seasoned host spearheading TikTok's livestream services, saw a revenue of 360 million RMB in total.

Celebrities

It is a time when the film and television industries eager to make adjustment, and many film stars and celebrities have changed their strategy from assisting influencers to personally selling goods through livestreams. The celebrities with diversiform characteristics, wide-reaching reputations and solidified fan bases are ideal to generate high conversion rates and consumer's optimism towards brand values. They deeply connect with brands and consumers, skilful in turning the advantage into their own commercial value and social influence. TV and film stars who possess certain fan bases or social influence, such as Li Xiang, Li Xiaolu, Liu Tao and Li Jing, have well facilitated the injection of outside capitals and traffic into the industry, transforming preliminary monetising methods into real industrial development, in rather imaginative ways, as well as bringing to fruition a unique ecosystem of "stars e-commerce" that consists of various livestream models. In the cooperation between the leading hosts such as Viya and Li Jiaqi and the traditional celebrities like Jing Boran and Kris Wu, the presence of stars in commercial livestreams has imperceptibly reshaped the industrial ecology, as well as changed livestream's reputation as but a vulgar form of entertainment in the public eye.

And what the celebrities have learned from influencers is how to mobilise the temperament of "humanisation", which is the opposite of the performance they were used to that is sarcastically regarded as robotic or attitudinising. It is the image of "friends" that has sprouted out of the celebrities' previous personas that used to be filled with superiority and then later altered by the celebrities themselves when participating in livestreams. Now, their reshaped, commoner personas contain plenty of private and personal traits, which are added to the concrete fan bases, the nationwide recognition and favourable reception from the media and the public alike, making it even easier for them to build trust and emotional bonds with audience, on the livestream platforms as their new stages where the physical distance between performers and audience is shortened. In short, it is now a normalcy the celebrities attempt to put on themselves the body languages and facial expressions of the influencers to be imagined as more approachable, even to best the influencers in this new manner of online marketing. By now, many of them have succeeded, and in the meantime brought about a perpendicular rise of the conversion rate in livestreaming e-commerce, with the aid of their rich experience in showing charming personalities.

Through community interaction, information sharing and digital entertainment consumption, commercial livestreams enhanced by certain scenes may create an environment of strong interaction, high-level immersion and a sense of liberalisation. When celebrities enter their livestream room, they behave differently than they do offline or on the screens. In the traditional way of acting that is reflected on a digital screen, there is no instant interaction between celebrities and audience, which highlights the differences in identities. Unlike that, the "star + livestream" model not only ignites the dual pleasure of audience's sense and emotion but also shortens the identity gap,[2] which was an improbability in the past. In the sense of livestreaming, a celebrity performing a certain role in a corresponding scene is a return of symbolic ritual, a motion painting with interactive landscape as canvas. If his/her vivid personality matches the brand image, a positive effect is triggered and the audience are led to believe the promoted product is favourable in appearance and quality alike, as with the celebrity's acting. Lin Yilun, for instance, who once was a popular singer, participated as a livestream host in the Food Festival (May 17) of 2020 and gave the audience a rather appealing performance. Lin harvested 167,941 orders from his livestreams, with the number of views exceeding 2.73 million and the volume of transaction over 11.4 million RMB.

Influencers

Having Bested numerous influencers stationed on China's e-commerce platforms, Viya and Li Jiaqi made themselves a pair of commercial megastars of 2020 with striking sales performances. In the single year, for fifty times were the two livestream hosts seen on Weibo's list of trending topics, surpassing most of the first-line celebrities. Extremely voguish as they were, Viya and Li made clear of that they would rather prefer the title "Internet marketer" than "celebrity" or "superstar", though for

[2] Huang Zhongjun, Jiang Zhihan, "A New Vanity Fair in the Consumer Era: A Study on Celebrity-Centered Commercial Livestreams", *Journal of School of Chinese Language and Culture, Nanjing Normal University*, Vol. 4, 2020.

the majority there were few differences. Nationwide, after all, they were deemed synonymous with conversion rate and financial success, just like the traditional stars, despite their emphasis on their hardworking and ordeal-conquering, and on that their successes were but skyscrapers built up bit by bit without shortcuts and beyond duplication. "There will never be another Li Jiaqi, I am what I am", that the celebrated marketer himself proudly asserted.

Zhang Dayi: The First Influencer in China

With over 12 million fans supplying incessant traffic on the Weibo platform, Zhang Dayi stays assuredly among the first echelon of Chinese online influencers. In 2016, Alibaba Group invested 300 million RMB in Ruhan Holdings, Zhang's influencer incubating company, and became its fourth-largest shareholder. The capital injection was even higher than the Ruhan's market value at the time, which demonstrated Alibaba's confidence and resolve since Ruhan was the only MCN organisation the group ever invested in. After the investment, Ruhan's market value soared to 3.132 billion RMB and the company was listed in the United States in March 2019. Now, it has on its payroll 113 influencers who own a total of 148 million fans, generating nearly 1 billion RMB as the company's annual revenue. Soon after, Zhang's story was vividly presented in the documentary *The Influencers*, a microcosm of thousands of influencers in China. Gilded with the working-hard-and-getting-reward kind of storytelling, Zhang soon became an inspirational icon of success and her most fruitful years were branded as "the era of Zhang Dayi". On the night when Ruhan was listed in America, the company received more than 3,000 messages, all from young women yearning for joining Ruhan to clone Zhang's prestige, holding in heart the motto they forged for their idol: "Large an army of rivals no matter how, Dayi shall always prevail".

Back when paper media still had a firm hold on the dissemination of entertaining information, Zhang never failed to seize the chance of gathering public attention by her glamorous photos radiating unique temperament printed on the front page of fashion magazines like *Vi Vi* and *Rayli*. During that time when Taobao was yet to dominate the market of online shopping, the frequent appearance of Zhang on fashion magazines recommending beauty brands was a powerful influence on young females which, to a rather large extent, shaped their recognition of fashion and the way they defined voguish attraction. "Rayli Girl" was Zhang's label in the early days, which lasted 8 years until she finalised her career as a fashion model, an occupation later depicted by herself of little enjoyment in some interviews. To pursue her own dreams, Zhang took a brave step and opened "My Wardrobe" on Taobao in 2014, her own online store that mainly sells women's clothing. The next year, the number of her Weibo fans soared from 250,000 to over 4 million, which well proved her competence to attract fans as an e-commerce practitioner. And when she owned more than 10 million fans and were recognised as a harbinger of China's influencer marketing, the expression "era of Zhang Dayi" seemed to be more persuasive. It was also the year when China's influencer-driven economy began to take off, which therefore was called "the first year of Internet influencer".

In 2016, Zhang Dayi expanded her fashion business and opened two new stores online, setting foot in lingerie and beauty products in addition to clothing. On the opening day of the beauty store, 20,000 lipsticks were sold in two hours. Meanwhile, she conducted her first livestream on Taobao and ended it with the number of views exceeding 413,000, which broke the record set by Liu Yan, a renowned actress and television presenter, whose most fruitful livestream received over 140,000 views. Availed by the record-breaking livestream that day, Zhang vented goods valued at 20 million RMB in two hours.

Evidently, Zhang Dayi was one of China's most eminent influencers before Viya and Li Jiaqi, judging by her fans' high level of activity and her remarkable capability of making sales and erecting topics, let alone she was the first Internet influencer to camp on the Taobao platform. However, what followed Zhang's acclaimed achievement was Taobao's strategy upgrading. The platform hoped not only to invest in the top influencers but also in the minor ones to boost profits in full scale. After the decision was made and the policies were released, the battles for traffic among influencers grew fiercer. The unexpected change jammed them all in a bottleneck and seeking out better ways to gather limited traffic became their top priority.

In 2018, Viya and Li Jiaqi created a commercial myth by making sales of merchandise worthy of over 10 million RMB in a few hours. Then, in the next year, the era led by Zhang Dayi was suddenly taken over. In March 2019, Zhang Dayi guested in Li Jiaqi's livestream room to promote her facial cleanser, and the livestream soon turned into Li's solo show, as the vigorous new star of e-commerce sold 10,000 units of Zhang's facial cleanser in mere 10 seconds. Later on the Double Eleven of the same year, Viya and Li Jiaqi continued their astounding performance, proving themselves Zhang's qualified successors. On the ranking of popular sellers on the day of Taobao's Double Eleven pre-sale, Viya ranked first with the number of views achieving 55.76 million, followed by Li Jiaqi's 336.58 million. Zhang Dayi was the fourth on the rank list behind Cherie, with a total of 20.39 million views, and failed to reach the same level as Viya and Li. Though it seemed that she has pasted her prime, Zhang's resolve has not been weakened as she still commits to her career as a livestream host by persistence, expecting for a breakthrough.

Li Jiaqi: China's Lipstick King

Li Jiaqi[3] graduated from Nanchang University, who never engaged in works related to his undergraduate major. Purely by chance as he said, he stepped into the beauty industry. Li started his career as a shopping guide of a L'Oréal shop in Nanchang. In the six years' practice on the frontline of sales, he learned plenty about how to satisfy consumers' needs and accumulated enough experience, which was fundamental for him to win the audience's trust with efficiency later as a livestream host. After L'Oréal, Li went to Shanghai and then signed a contract with Mei ONE. As one of the earliest MCNs that joined forces with Taobao in the field of livestreaming e-commerce, Mei ONE cooperated with L'Oréal in the latter's "Project Buying Assistant", and Li was appointed as an online buying assistant to Taobao's livestream platform.

Li Jiaqi started livestreaming in November 2019. With the experience he gathered in the early days, he served his consumers and fans charmingly and reputably, running lipstick trails on himself and teaching them how to make the best use of the products. After three years' extraordinary endeavour, Li stood out as a top-ranking livestream host who never failed to provide heavy transaction volume. During the Double Eleven of 2018, he once sold 15,000 lipsticks in 5 minutes using Taobao's livestream services and later ended his show in the shopping festival with a turnover exceeding 330 million RMB, bested his competitors all and broke the domestic record. Then, in 2019, he set a Guinness record for "the most lipstick applications to models in 30 seconds". Between October 20 and

[3] Li Jiaqi, "Li Jiaqi's First Public Speaking: My Methodology and Three Things to Do in the Future", WeChat Official Account "Xinbang", released on November 18, 2019. https://mp.weixin.qq.com/s/XbQYG3uflsaALrnjhanmqA.

21, 2020, he livestreamed twice and concluded with a PV reaching 233 million RMB and a GMV close to 5.14 billion RMB. His popularity was still soaring.

Throughout 2020, Li never stopped livestreaming for a day and conducted 389 livestreams in total, more than 10 business teams waiting in line for a chance to collaborate with him on an average day. Till today, the stunning efficiency appears to be a requisite for his success. What his team submits to him are mostly numbers abstracted from products for choice, such as data of quantity, original price, preferential price and commission rate. Averagely, he needs to judge whether he promotes a product or not in a second. It has amazed many that he is competent enough to consider both work efficiency and product quality, and meanwhile introduces to his fans dozens of goods with all-inclusive information, in his four-hour livestreams every day. Aside from his astounding vigour and vitality however, it is not so obscure that one of his keys to success is his marketing strategies for different groups that he categorised his fans into by purchase power, level of income and social status. He is always well versed in the matters concerning consumers' needs, especially young women's, as a benefaction of his early-built insight into the beauty industry. Nevertheless, both the factors neither slights the value of his many years of practice in livestreaming and his insistence on beauty products, nor belittles his inspiriting exploits, which has broadened everyone's horizons in the e-commerce industry. And above all, he has formed his own style in his area of expertise, which he himself is quite proud of.

Li described his livestreaming style simply as a mixture of three words, as in "integrity", "genuineness" and "practicality". For his fans, his soothing voice, fast speech speed and highly distinguishable body languages are inspirationally enjoyable, in which they always see his passion and faith in everyday life and find themselves encouraged. Li's iconic slogans in livestreams, such as "oh my god", "all girls go for it, just go for it" and "your DEVIL is here" are never short of exaggeration and even rich of ostentation, for people who think of him as more likely a talk-show-style zany, or put it moderately, a garrulous guest in a minor entertaining reality show. Anyway, Li's highly contentious performing style is part of what made him the first extremely productive IP of Mei ONE. Back in 2019, Li had already made his future plans, mainly taking account into the following three points: first, keep up the good work online, or "go on putting up the best of the bests for my likers" as he announced; second, keep up the good work offline, or more explicitly, found a retailer of beauty products featuring multiple brands, like Sephora, to gather all sorts of merchandise promoted by him and to serve customers in a "get-it-while-it-lasts" way of marketing, as he believes the future marketing model of e-commerce will still lie in the blend of online and offline shopping experiences, at least for the foreseeable future; third, build a Chinese brand that is worldly renowned, to fulfil his own dream.

Viya: Taobao's Trump Card

Judging by Viya's[4] genial and approachable performance in her livestream room, it is not imaginable for everyone that the path she walked from an unknown to an e-commerce star was neither sunlit nor smooth. She started as a model and then opened a clothing store offline. In the following years, she expanded her business from Beijing to Xi'an and later to Guangzhou, with no lack of capital deficits and overstock of commodities in the meantime, each step accompanied by adversities. After a long-lasting baptism of painstaking, she acquired self-confidence and the radiant semblance before her millions of fans.

In March 2016, Taobao started the first trial of their mobile shopping platform, namely Taobao Live, indicating that the water-testing period of livestreaming e-commerce had come. At the beginning, 80% of the platform's users were women interested in cosmetics, apparels, sports apparatuses and beauty products, everything the platform was featured with. Due to the increase in demand, Taobao realised that were they to further upgrade their intelligent services, what they needed was a "matrix" of livestream hosts rather than a single powerful official livestream account. It was when the frustrated Viya was invited by Taobao as one of the many first-timers of livestreaming e-commerce and decided to make a career in the newborn industry. In May 2016, she presented her first livestream and soon proved to be a game changer.

[4] Viya, a famous Chinese anchor with e-commerce. In May 2016, Viya officially became an anchor of Taobao Live, and four months later, her sales volume reached 100 million. In 2018, Viya started to devote herself to public welfare live broadcast, helping to fight poverty through e-commerce, and by far has driven the sales of agricultural products in poor areas of China to nearly 30 million. By 2020, she has been considered as one of the most influential business women in China. At 00:00 of October 21, 2020, Viya set a record of making 600 million yuan's worth of sales with a single link, as well as a GMV that reached 5.32 billion yuan in the Double.

After learning that it was essential a livestream host's services accorded with both the customers' needs and the platform's rules of traffic distribution, she pioneered a series of experiments such as building a livestream team, offering fashion advices, trying featured apparels on herself and holding clothes' demonstrations in a fashion show style. By doing this, she converted herself from a sheer sharer of content into a value creator and a public relations professional. Suffice to say, she was among the earliest adventurers who boldly shaped Taobao's e-commerce ecosystem.

On October 10, 2016, Viya's livestream room generated a daily revenue exceeding 70 million RMB, setting a domestic new record. It was a testament to the monetising power of Viya's livestreams and a sign of a new tide's surging as well, which was to flood people's daily lives soon enough since commercial livestreams already shook the foundation of traditional e-commerce. As one of the first participants in livestreaming e-commerce, Viya survived and also exceptionally profited from the time of change by finding a firm foothold as well as adapting to the radically changed rules in the abrupt market evolution. Since 2016, she has been among the top-ranking livestream hosts on Taobao, bestowed honorary titles including "TOP 10 Most Commercially Valuable Livestream Hosts", "TOP 10 Most Popular Hosts", "TOP 3 Most Popular Livestream Girls", which manifested her irreplaceable commercial value for the platform. In 2019, Viya began to include foreign products in her livestreams and later was awarded the title of "One-Belt-One-Road Ambassador for Commodity Recommendation" by the Ministry of Commerce of Thailand. Taobao's Tmall also awarded her as "Global Products Recommendation Officer" and "National E-Commerce Connoisseur" in the same year. By now, she has close to 5 million followers on Taobao and plans to extend her booming business to the world.

Xin Ba, "a Host for the People"

Xin Ba, whose real name is Xin Youzhi, was born in 1990 in a mountain village at the foot of Lesser Khingan, a mountain range in Northeast China. To get rid of poverty, Xin Ba went through a lot as a teenager, which polished his commercial sense, though not enough for his early tries. Before he started livestreaming, he had failed four times to build his own business. Almost stressed out, he chose to go overseas and take his chances in Japan. By coincidence, he then saw business opportunities in Kao's diapers through a careful study of the product. After that, he made up his mind and began to stock up and sell the Kao diapers, hoping for enough initial capital for some more ambitious plans. Those experiences in his early years might have narrowed the emotional gap between him and ordinary people, making it easier for him to win the goodwill of his fans. Xin Ba understood this very well and thus always referred to himself "a son of farmers, a host for the people" ever since he started livestreaming on Kwai, which is partly why a good many of his audience live or grew up in rural regions, regardless of age, gender and occupation.

For Xin Ba, Kwai's livestream platform is not only a digital workplace, but also a springboard that launched him from a lower class to the enviable wealth, and a patron he has repaid with generosity. In 2019, the income generated from Xin Ba's livestreams totalling 13.3 billion RMB, close to one quarter of the platform's GMV this year. Beyond that, he also made himself a shining icon for Kwai's public image by acting as an energetic provider of welfare, a zealous activist of the government's overwhelming anti-poverty project. It appears that Xin Ba has never been a miser when it comes to charitable causes, who once gifted 818,000 RMB to the forest firefighters of Xichang, a small city in Southwest China, and 6 million RMB to Zhong Nanshan Foundation who dedicates to medical research, plus a total of 5 million RMB donated to his home village by Lesser Khingan. He also fully invested in the founding of a primary school in Daliangshan, a county in Southwest China that suffered from extreme poverty. For the government, of course, Xin Ba's charitable deeds were politically profitable and thus a series of medals and honorary titles, such as the medal of "Honourable Youth of Heilongjiang Province" and the "Ambassador for Anti-Poverty and Farmer's Prosperity", were bestowed on the young man in succession. Clearly, the "host for the people" benefited much from the dedication-encouraging political orientation and vice versa, though the honeymoon phase proved not to be so long-running. In early 2020, Xin Ba was accused of selling counterfeit edible bird's nests and soon banned by all the livestream platforms in China as the commercial fraud was verified. Two months later when the ban was over, he returned to Kwai with his old generosity, presenting to the fans various costly gifts such as gold bars, mao-tai, iPhones and a fleet of 30 BMWs. Xin Ba was resolved to win back the loyalty of the audience with his wealth, judging by the livestream in which he mostly did was hand out "red pockets", one turn after another. It was more or less 1 million RMB each turn cost him.

It stays true till today that if you wish to be competitive in the livestream industry, you ought to make your supply chain enduring, resilient and flexible, a complete system with all-round power. Fairly speaking, therefore, Xin Ba's main recipe for success in livestreaming e-commerce is that he has a complete supply chain, other than his generosity. The efficiently functioning system was operated by a crew of 100 marketing specialists, with Xi Ban being a sort of a dictatorial team leader who always makes the final decision on whether a product is to be put on the show or not, and leaves the price, discount, customer service and matters of logistics for the system to adjust. Through this efficiency labour-dividing procedure, the host and his teammates together form a professional and standardised supply chain, knowledgeable of every piece of information regarding production process, manufacturing cost, accessories, etc., which is also one of the reasons why Xin Ba usually seems bold enough to offer his fans a highly preferable price, "a price for the people", that his competitors dare not provide due to the lack of information.

As of July 31, 2020, according to the data collected during the third China Brand Economy Summit, Viya was still on the top of the list of the most prosperous livestream hosts by revenue, who earned 2.03 billion RMB through livestreaming in the last 30 days, followed by Li Jiaqi who saw 1.403 billion RMB. And it was Xin Ba who ranked the third, with a monthly income of 526 million RMB generated from his commercial livestreams.

Entrepreneur Hosts: The Dual-IP-Driven Strategy

Aside from Internet influencers and traditional celebrities, there were a good many of corporate leaders who have adapted the changed marketing environment of e-commerce as well and made themselves part-time livestream hosts. Some of the most renowned ones, such as Dong Mingzhu who runs Gree, Liang Jianzhang who administers Ctrip and Luo Yonghao, CEO of Hammer Technology, appear to be as much influential when livestreaming as they are in the real world, drawing a great deal of public attention. As practised commanders and marketing veterans, those entrepreneurs saw from the beginning the huge business opportunities in livestreaming e-commerce and captured them without hesitation. Relying on their long established personal influence, they have introduced into livestream e-commerce the marketing model that combines the leverages of themselves and their brands to make the products better known, enlarge the sales and tame the critiques, known as the dual-IP-driven strategy.

On May 10, 2020, Dong Mingzhu gave her first commercial livestream on Kwai and earned over 100 million RMB in half an hour with only three products promoted. The income doubled 70 minutes later, and the three-hour livestream ended with a total revenue of 310 million RMB. According to Dong, Gree made 350 million RMB in 2019 by selling electric appliances, which means Dong made an amount of money that almost equals her company's total revenue in the last year, by livestreaming for three hours. Lei Jun, CEO of Xiaomi Group, also had a resounding success in his first livestreaming show that was watched over 500 million times by more than 50.53 million viewers on TikTok. In the end, Lei left his livestream room with a total of 570,000 purchase orders.

The table below shows some of the most active entrepreneur hosts in livestreaming e-commerce and their occupations, platforms, total numbers of views as of the end of 2020 (Table 1).

Vocaloid Hosts: Breaking Dimensional Barriers

On April 21, 2020, Li Jiaqi for the first time teamed up in his livestream with Luo Tianyi, a Chinese vocaloid singer. Then, ten days later on May 1, the vocaloid attended a livestream in Tmall's Youth Laboratory, a livestream room operated by Taobao. The number of views reached 2.7 million and more than 2 million viewers presented gifts to the vocaloid. Other vocaloid stars such as Yuezheng Ling, Hatsune Miku and Noonoouri have also begun to get involved in livestreaming e-commerce. It is impracticable so far that a vocaloid conducts commercial livestreams independently due to technical restriction. Still, their connection with anime/manga lovers, who mainly are young people born later than 1995, has already led to the break of "dimensional limits" and a rise of livestreaming e-commerce's popularity among the younger generation. As of 2019, there were over 490 million anime/manga fans in China, about 64% of them junior citizens born after 1995. As time goes on, the younger generation will soon be the main force of consumption, and yet the bridge connecting livestreaming e-commerce and the anime/manga culture favoured by a good many of them is far from a completion.

Table 1 This chart mainly illustrates CEOs of well-known Chinese large companies from different industries involved in the live-streaming e-commerce industry, these presentations contain sales categories and market revenues

CEO	*Video views*	*Industry*	*Platform*
Liang Jianzhang, chairman of Ctrip	8 livestreaming events generated more than 2.5 billion yuan's revenue	Travel industry	multiple platforms
Yu Dunde, CEO of Tuniu	More than 20,000 people watched the show, with more than 40,000 comments	Travel industry	TikTok
Chen Gang, CEO of Qunar	More than 3.8 million people watched the show with more than 16 million yuan's revenue generated	Travel industry	Kwai
Wang Yu, chairman of Spring Airlines	More than 8 million people watched the show	Travel & Civil aviation	TikTok
Chen Xiaodong, CEO of Yintai	More than 220,000 people watched the show	Shopping industry	Taobao
5 CEOs of Macalline	More than 1 million people watched the show	Furniture industry	Taobao
Huang Wei, CEO of Zhuanzhuan	The show sold more than 700 phone units, generating nearly 4 million yuan's revenue	Second-hand trading platform	Zhuanzhuan APP
Sun Chunlai, funder of Linqingxuan	More than 60,000 people watched the show with more than 400,000 yuan's revenue generated	Beauty makeup industry	Taobao
Qian Jinbo, CEO of Red Dragonfly	The sales of the flagship store increased 136%	Clothing industry	Taobao Live
Li Shujun, CEO of Septwolves	The total number of interactions exceeded 130,000, and the turnover was 380,000 yuan	Clothing industry	WeChat small Application

(continued)

Table 1 (continued)

CEO	*Video views*	*Industry*	*Platform*
Hou Yi, President of Freshhema	6 million Hubei crayfish and 500,000 Hubei oranges were sold in the show	Agricultural products/E-commerce	Taobao Live
Liang Linhe, chairman of Sany Heavy Truck	186 heavy trucks were sold, with a sales volume of 50 million yuan	Heavy machinery	TikTok
Xu Zhihua, CEO of Peak Sports	The show generated more 50 million yuan's revenue	Sport	Tmall
Cheng Cheng, CEO of Care Daily	The transaction amount was 6.12 million	Infant & Mom	Tencent Live
Dong Mingzhu, CEO of Gree	The transaction amount was 225,300	Household appliance industry	TikTok
Wang Cheng, CEO of TCL	10,000 units were sold within one hour	Household appliance industry	JD
Zhang Jiayin, CEO of McDonald's China	About a million people were watching the show during the peak hours	Food industry	Bilibili
Luo Yonghao, founder of Smartisan Technology	The transaction amount was 139 million yuan	Household appliance industry	TikTok

It goes without saying that vocaloid hosts will always have an edge over human hosts, as they can livestream for as long as they remain functional, without worrying about time, fatigue or labour cost, which, convenient as it is inherently, is rather suitable for vitalising the fan-based economy, let alone the air of newness and wonder the new audience will always sense when they see the vividly humanised computer programmes.

With vocaloid hosts joining the business, now we have seen a more complex e-commerce ecosystem, in which fan-based economic models are diversifying as much as the marketing value of vocaloid IPs are enriched. That being the case, however, to elevate vocaloid hosts to the complete independence from human assistance and a high level of performing humanlike facial expressions and physical actions, which offer audience with a more vivid experience of immersion, time is still needed.

2 Host-Audience Interaction

2.1 Preheating before Livestreaming: Unbolt the Door for Massive Traffic

A strong preheating before livestreaming is always effective for hosts to attract the attention of their fans, a necessity on every shopping occasions in China when commercial livestreams are to be organised, like every year's Double Eleven and Double Twelve. Generally speaking, social networking sites and short video platforms such as WeChat's Moments, Channels, official accounts and other major social networks like Weibo are all regular carriers of strong preheating in many forms, including posters, audio and video materials, image-text combinations and the like, in order to present content and information concerning promotional products, celebrities invited, livestreaming time schedules and product categories. Specifically, the forms of preheating can be divided into two types: preheating in advance and preheating in prologue.

In the interview executed by this book's research team, the interviewees, namely the top-ranking host Li Jing[5] and her operation executives, explained in detail the procedure of releasing a short teaser video with product information before livestreaming. Li Jing, who has changed her profession from a TV host to a livestream host, is to check thirty-odd varieties of products that the selection team has finalised, and in the process, she must constantly think about one question: how to encourage the audience to make a buying decision within 3–5 minutes? The host must use her experience to quickly determine which products are of interest to different age groups and pick them out for preheating. On the next step, the publicity team is to record promotional videos for the products. The videos are usually made directly on smartphones and each contains a one-sentence recommendation from the host, focusing on the product's highlights and special features. Fifteen minutes before livestreaming, the team is done releasing the videos on all of Li's social

[5] Li Jing is a Chinese TV show host and founder of LeBee.com, who used to work as a show host in China Beijing TV and China Central Television. In 2005, she established China's first online video interactive talk show "Quiet Distance", which is Li's only programme named after herself. In 2006, Li Jing hosted the entertainment programme "Entertainment hot pot". In 2008, she founded Lepi.com, a celebrity-centered platform mainly regarding Li's own brand "Jingjia" as well as beauty-oriented e-commerce. In 2009, "Quiet Distance" was renamed "Very Quiet Distance".

networking accounts to warm up the fans for the incoming livestream. The preheating videos effectively fuel viewers to make a quick purchase decision once the livestream begins, and resultantly, massive traffic rushes in and forms a "private traffic pool" for the host.

2.2 Host's Self-Empowerment: The Shining Personas

The reason why the top influencers' personal IPs are able to stand still, as well as to achieve the effect of breaking the barriers among social circles, is related to their vivid personas. Each KOL's persona and style determines that behind each of them there are a certain group of vertical fans. Based on their emotional connection with KOLs, fans have a higher trust in marketing messages. If a KOL's persona is distinguishable and clear, her emotional connection with audience will be strong, the livestream's content will be genial and natural, and consequently, the marketing conversion will rise.

In actual cases, a host's discernible wording is rather helpful in promoting a product. This phenomenon can be explained by the "Goebbels effect". Joseph Goebbels stated that "a lie repeated a hundred times becomes the truth". This statement has been introduced in the field of communication and led to a standardised definition of the "Goebbels effect". A message is sent to an individual in an implicit, indirect way, and the individual receives the message unconsciously and thus reacts in a certain psychological or behavioural manner. There is a fat probability that a livestream host's wording achieves "Goebbels effect", simply by repetition and some influential phrases that stimulate audience's consumption behaviour. For example, Li Jiaqi's high-frequency phrases used in his livestreams (such as the highly distinguishable "OMG" and "All girls go for it!") are rich in regional features and also labels of individuality. Those phrases are carved in audience' hearts and minds over and again, and the audience cannot resist but to be reminded of Li whenever the phrases appear. That is to say, a host's deeply trademarked wording may unleash a kind of charm, inducing among audience a psychological projection of dependency.

The cultivation of Li Jiaqi as an absurdly profitable IP is basically a blend of sincerity, acting and crowd control that establishes memory points through certain wordings, body languages and a large-scale fan-effect to create mass communication. Irving Goffman's famous "mimesis theory" in his *The Presentation of Self in Everyday Life* argues that in the big stage of society, everyone to some extent is doing performance, i.e. self-presentation that is not fully authentic, and that people perform within the framework of performance formed by various social norms.[6] The hosts use elements of performance to influence audience through unique preset persona. Li Jiaqi's concise words and extremely rendering tone, which are also symbolised, assume the role of disseminating information, create a consumer domain and use generalised publicity to make audience agree with what is being promoted. Relatively speaking, what a livestream a host presents in a commercial livestream is an idealised performance in a corresponding scene, carefully choreographed and rehearsed, using elements of performance to influence the consumer, with a certain persona building and merchandising as the purpose, which is as much embellished as the content itself.

2.3 Interactive Entertainment: A Stress-Relieving Revelry

In livestreaming e-commerce, celebrities and top-ranking hosts usually maintain high-frequency interaction with their fans and audience. The incessant interaction attracts fans' attention non-stop and reduces the momentary loss of their scarce attention. A livestream room is not only a host's working space, but also a spiritual habitat for the fans. It is a specific scene for fans and alike, a "second world" detached from real life, where hosts and fans talk to each other on an equal footing, breaking down identity barriers, sharing the sense of empathy, gaining a collective identity, coming together in a highly homogeneous consciousness and generating social unity through strong interaction. This typical phenomenon fits in with the theory of the revelry first proposed by the critic Bakhtin in the 1960s in his *Dostoevsky's Problems of Poetics*. Bakhtin pointed out that the phenomenon of the orgy exists in the "second world" of human life, where the orgy is collective and universal in nature, where class restrictions are removed and common people can enjoy equality and freedom, reveal their inner feelings and give vent to their hidden emotions.

So, how is the "second world" constructed between hosts and audience? How is the emotional bond between hosts and audience forged? We know livestreaming e-commerce is a combination of consumption and entertainment. In the strong interaction day after day, not only hosts have

[6] Irving Goffman, *The Presentation of Self in Everyday Life*, trans. by Feng Gang, Beijing University Press, April 2008.

been reshaping their identities, but the fans have also realised a renewal of themselves. Hosts go from being product promoters to accompanying fans in their changes, concerned with their real-life needs, relieving emotional anxiety and even tailoring friendship. When audience enter a livestream room, they are removed from their realistic frame of self and able to reshape their image and identity. In the case of Viya, she affectionately refers to her fans as "Viya's women", understanding their concerns as if they were actual friends, increasing mutual trust and narrowing the emotional gap. The term "Viya's women" has also become a symbol for Viya, representing a token of belonging to the community and a high level of emotional identity. Genuine or not, that only Viya knows.

3 Creating Hit Products

3.1 Acquaintance-Based Promotion: Hosts in the Two-Step Flow

Livestream hosts' aim is to bring about high conversion rate and large sales volume, based on the attributes and quality of products. The triple advantages of convincing quality, abundant traffic and loud brand voice form the competitiveness of leading hosts. But it is relatively difficult to ensure the three factors at the same time.

In her livestream room, Viya keeps telling her fans, intentionally or not, that her relatives and acquaintances are users of her promotional products. "See this facial mask? Ask my team if it's great. Gosh, all my staff are crazy about it! And my family too. This is THE facial mask I'm using at home. My husband too, even my mom. Know what? I've just got one for my daughter". Starting from user experiences of the people around her that are ordinary customers, the host makes an acquaintance-based promotion, which is effective on gaining audience's trust. Imperceptibly, the audience's sense of trust is enhanced, and their loyalty is improved.

According the "two-step flow" model of communication introduced by Lazarsfeld in *The People's Choice*, ideas flow from mass media to opinion leaders, and from them to a wider population. In the process, opinion leaders blend their own interpretation of information in with the original content.[7] As the intermedia in the two-step flow, opinion leaders are rooted in a complex network of social relations. These are the people

[7] Paul F. Lazarsfeld, *The People's Choice*, trans. by Tang Qian, Beijing: China Renming University Press, June 2012.

who have strong interaction with each other rather than being isolated. In livestreaming e-commerce, hosts assume the role of opinion leaders that are usually thought to be individuals with hyper-normally charming personality and all-round abilities, who therefore are regarded as higher in social status, capable of influencing others' minds. Now, it has become a trend in livestreaming e-commerce that the "opinion leaders", mainly the professional livestream hosts, perform before audience in their livestream rooms as product presenters and also purchase encouragers.

3.2 The Balance between High Quality and Low Price

According to the "Report on Consumption of Livestreaming E-commerce" released by Beijing Consumers Association, the main reasons for consumers to participate in livestreaming e-commerce are cheap price and friendly merchandise display. More than half of those surveyed inclined to choose cheaper products, while 44.56% of them made their choices by product presentation. Besides that, 26.32% of the respondents followed the majority's choice, 29.12% performed impulse purchases, and 21.56% took recommendations from livestream hosts. The report also shows that quality and price are the two most decisive factors for the buyers, since 63.86% of the surveyed claimed they value good quality and 63.51% of them value low price. On other aspects, 23.56% of the respondents made their decision by the fame of livestream hosts, 21.75% by their expression of livestream platforms and 14.04% by the size of retailers.

Such being the case, "good quality and cheap price" seems to be a pair of necessities for a hit product in livestream e-commerce. To achieve the first goal as in "good quality", product selection plays a crucial role. Many MCN organisations and top hosts have their own product selection teams. Based on seasons, consumers' needs and fans' preference, they evaluate market demand and make product selection. To create differentiation, a selected product ought to hit the pain points of sales target as soon as the product's position in the market is found. Meantime, the prerequisite, namely "good quality", must be set up by differentiating the product from standardised, congeneric merchandise in the market. Top hosts such as Viya and Li Jiaqi have clear standards when it comes to product selection, for they obviously prefer to recommend products that are mass-popular, of light-service and priced from 30 to 50 RMB.

Though the competitiveness of Viya's sales team lies in "cost-effective", repeatedly promoting a small batch of products in a limited time also proves to be their main strategy. The team's objective can be described as "sell out in a single round + give them another shot". Normally, products are not to be presented all at once, since one small batch at a time is much easier to be snapped up, and Viya has always asked her team "can we get some more" each time after a sold-out, in order to evoke an atmosphere of low price and large sales. Without audience's awareness, an air of buying competition has been bred. Consequently, audience are inclined to herd mentality, which is magnified by the host's dramatic performance and swiftly dominates a wide population, and impulse purchases are thus made in excitement. This is the common gimmick of many top-ranking hosts on livestream platforms.

From the perspective of economics, the incentive theory suggests that anticipations can be accomplished mainly through rewarding or punishing. Looking back at Viya's case, specific goals are constantly set to affect audience's needs, and consumption behaviours are gradually strengthened as well as maintained during the process. Meanwhile, price incentive is also applied to encourage the audience to make purchases. All this makes it easy for Viya to make profits in a large scale, since neither traffic supply nor conversation rate is to be worried in her livestream room. Moreover, retailers cooperating with her are always willing to offer more preferable discounts if purchase orders are sufficient, which also helps create a precondition of "low price".

4 Sense of Immersion

4.1 The blend of Scene and Experience: Product's Symbolic Value

Livestreaming e-commerce is a chain that links people with products and consumption scenes, thus requiring experienced hosts, high-quality products and suitable scene designs. As Zhang Yong, board chairman and CEO of Alibaba, once said, the consumption scenes and marketing scenes have been changing, and livestream host such as "lipstick king" represents a new trend of consumption. Such changes behind people, products and scenes reflect the changes of business. Scenes created in a livestream room are connected with promotional products in a specific way. They make the product images clearer to the consumers and more consistent with the price through scenic expression and arrangement, which concern vertical audience, pain points, the scenes themselves and other means, and may effectively cultivate consumption behaviours.

To expand the range of target audience, the top hosts usually implant multiple product trial scenes into livestreaming e-commerce. Focusing on the main selling points of the products, they in advance design various scenes due to user experience, including that of daily life, leisure and entertainment, amusement and brain-racking, and even sci-fi future, so that the scenic effects will permeate the products' actual effects, thereby offering the sense of immersion. In Li Jiaqi's commercial livestreams, for instance, beauty product promotion takes up a great proportion of the business, and Li's female fans prefer spending most of their energy on self-review and improving personal charm. Li will thereby lead his fans to an imagination of future time-space scene where he can build images of charming females that his fans dream to be, putting them in the hope of becoming ideal selves.

Along with the gradual maturity of livestreaming e-commerce, Internet celebrities nowadays can arrange livestream scenes in plenty of locales, such as sales bases, shopping malls and farms, instead of being limited to their online livestream rooms. This new way of livestreaming is vividly called "walk-streaming", meaning the hosts do their jobs while walking around locales of reality, which can help reinforce audience' experience of three-dimensional image and make them feel more on-site. In 2018, a host named "Xiang Xi Jiu Mei" (meaning "the ninth little sis of western Hunan") cooperated with some fruit growers and made 400,000 yuan out of their unsalable kiwi in two days, plus 1,000,000 kg of oranges in thirteen days. And a peach grower named Chen Zhihua living in Xikou Town, Fenghua City, once failed to sell his large stock of peaches, while a group of fifteen livestream hosts joined the business and 3,000 kg of peaches were sold out in an hour, which would have been left rotten in the fields. According to relevant information, during the Double Twelve shopping festival of 2018, some of Taobao hosts livestreamed for 12 days straight in Wuhan's Northern Hankou Clothing Town, Huzhou's Zhili Children's Clothing Town, Haining's Leather Town, Jingdezhen Ceramics workshops and other places. The sales volume of each major industrial base increased by two times on average.

These cases have proved the feasibility of boosting conversion rate through scene switching in livestreaming e-commerce. The reason is that scenes have symbolic value. When audience participate in different scenes, their needs for products or services will be different as well. On the other hand, scenes can also decide the symbolic values of relevant products, which change with the variation of context. This makes it rather important to confirm the symbolic meaning of certain products. Moreover, a scene created in a commercial livestream happens to be a combination of the product itself and the image of product usage, thus able to describe the abstract concept implanted in the product through specific scenes as thoroughly as possible, such as concepts regarding the product's target users, usage scenes and pain points. So as a result, the product's signifier and signified will be accord with each other to the full extent, and in such context, the symbolic meaning will be specified and specialised. The host, in addition, will also put in the product more symbolic meanings, like female audience will be offered a meaning of silently demonstrating their social attribute and fashion taste when buying a certain kind of lipstick, which is also a deed of seeking acceptance. This sort of consumption is no longer limited to material meanings, but more like in the realm of symbolic value.

4.2 Platform Empowerment and Resource Preference

Platforms that livestreaming e-commerce relies on include networks of different attributes. Various sorts of platforms, such as e-commerce platforms focusing on the circulation of commodities, social networking platforms regarding interpersonal communication in cyberspace and Internet platforms with attributes of the entertainment economy, have all shown a trend of extension to livestreaming e-commerce. Benefiting from the empowerment of AI, VR, AR, MR and other new technologies, the immersive and on-site experience offered by livestreaming e-commerce will grow more intelligent, and the underlying technology supports for the interaction of celebrities and fans will be more abundant. Such being the case, what kinds of resources, no matter of Internet traffic, monetisation channels, high-quality products and brand voice, will be capable of empowering the coexistence of effectiveness and reliability, as well as helping create top-level livestream hosts? On different platforms, there are different answers, which lead to different strategy principles that are to be discussed in the next chapter.

In livestreaming e-commerce, platforms' huge power of monetarisation is effective to help livestream hosts create high conversion rates sustainably. With the accelerating progress of media integration, cross-screen linkage of large and small devices, borderless experience of consumption scenes, technology empowerment has broken the barriers of e-commerce's traditional modes. The digital era not only gives platforms a sense of achievement, but also stimulates their strong demand for high profits. The demand needs livestreaming e-commerce to be the essence of support and inevitably relies on the ultra-high conversation rates created by livestream hosts. This will result in high proportion of traffic and resources inclining towards top-notch hosts, in whom the platforms have seen more possibilities than ever.

CHAPTER 4

Livestreaming E-Commerce Platforms in China: Types and Strategies

Abstract This chapter gives a comprehensive introduction to main livestreaming e-commerce platforms in China and their strategy principles. In general, Taobao Live and Buy Together are typical e-commerce-oriented platforms, while TikTok and Kwai can be defined as social networking livestream platforms. Taobao Live has reached the traffic ceiling and needs to increase the activeness of user engagement, which demands better livestream content and more varieties of merchandise. The advantages of Kwai include large-scale traffic monetisation, strong support for business partners and carefree core customers, but Kwai has an obvious disadvantage in the supply chain. Different platforms have different strategies. This chapter also analyses some representative cases of livestreaming e-commerce enterprises like Qianxun Group, the MCN agency behind top livestreamer Viya.

Keywords E-commerce platforms · Traffic monetisation · Core customers · User engagement

1 Industrial Chain of Livestreaming E-Commerce

Generally, a typical industrial chain of livestreaming e-commerce includes three layers. Those who form the topmost layer are brand owners,

R. Si, *China Livestreaming E-commerce Industry Insights*,
https://doi.org/10.1007/978-981-16-5344-5_4

merchants and manufacturers, mainly in charge of product supply and livestream sponsorship. The middle layer consists of MCN agencies, livestream hosts and livestream platforms. MCN agencies' work is to produce and organise livestream content, as well as to choose supplier and products for consideration, and leave supportive services, traffic management and monetisation to livestream platforms. And livestream hosts, naturally, are those who directly conduct livestreams. The bottom layer belongs to audience, who are expected to make purchases of merchandise recommended by livestream hosts through services provided by livestream platforms, making monetisation come true.

As an important link between the topmost layer and the bottom one, livestream platforms can be divided into two types, namely e-commerce-oriented platforms and social networking livestream platforms. The first type is originally built based on the e-commerce ecology, which can be used for both commercial livestreams and non-profit ones, and allows users to make direct purchases while watching livestreams without any intermediate step. The second type, on the other hand, is built based on the logic of social networking, with commercial livestream service as part of business expansion; users are to be transferred to another platform to finalise purchases after they are convinced by livestream hosts. In general, Taobao Live and Buy Together are typical e-commerce-oriented platforms, while TikTok and Kwai can be defined as social networking livestream platforms.

1.1 Taobao Live

Overview

As one of the oldest e-commerce-oriented platforms, Taobao Live in many regards is leading China's livestreaming e-commerce industry. As of 2019, it had accumulated over 400 million users and the annual GMV had totalled 200 billion RMB. By then, the booming business had kept the platform's turnover growth above 150% for three consecutive years. On Double Eleven of 2019, Taobao Live's livestream service generated a daily revenue of nearly 20 billion RMB, with more than half of the merchants stationed on the platform who conducted livestreams on that day. In the same year, the viewing time of Taobao Live livestreams was more than 30 minutes per capita, and a core user's daily active time was close to an hour averagely. About 65% of users who were directed to shopping pages by livestreams made purchases. At the same time, there were more than 1,000 MCN organisations certified by Alibaba, Taobao's parent company, and over 400 of them have installed more than 10 livestream hosts. By now, aside from Taobao Live itself, the Taobao-owned applications that have 600 million monthly active users in total also offer several access for users to get to the livestreams on Taobao Live, such as the homepages of Taobao, Weitao and many of the most popular stores on the applications.

Taobao Live has two unique advantages. The first is that it relies on the millions of Tmall merchants and the tens of millions of Taobao merchants to make Alibaba's supply chain fully function, and the second is that it has produced enough experienced and celebrated hosts who keep drawing massive amount of Internet traffic to the platform.

Development Process

Taobao's exploration of livestreaming e-commerce began in March 2016 with the trial operations of Taobao Live and Tmall Live. Two months later in May, Taobao Live officially went online, whose livestream hosts were mostly influencers and celebrities. One year later in 2017, Taobao Live and Tmall Live merged, making Taobao Live the only livestream platform subordinate to Taobao, and the rise of ordinary hosts was following. During the Double Twelve shopping festival in 2018, the transaction volume generated by Taobao Live increased by 160% compared with the same period in 2017. At the beginning of 2019, the Taobao Live application was officially launched before the Chinese Spring Festival with a market goal to earn 500 billion RMB in the next three years. In the same year, merchants that used Taobao's livestream service tripled as more than 1,000 MCN organisations joined Taobao Live. On the day of Double Eleven in 2019, Taobao Live's GMV reached 20 billion RMB.

Characteristics

The Obvious Matthew Effect

At present, Taobao Live is almost dominated by the most famed livestream hosts and MCN organisations. The top ten MCN organisations account for nearly 30% of the Internet traffic and 80% of the GMV. From the data released on Double Eleven, 2019, it is easy to see that the top hosts seized most of the traffic that flew to the platform, while the minor hosts' share was cut in half. During the shopping festival, 30% of the platform's GMV was generated from Viya's livestream room, and 20% was from Li Jiaqi's. Most likely the obvious Matthew effect will last long on Taobao Live, since it is easy for top hosts like Viya and Li to profit from a wider area of the market and to offer even larger discounts, in virtue of the ever-increasing inflow of traffic. No doubt, those traffic harvesters have firmly ensured the completion of the platform's GMV targets. However, how to have more active users for ordinary hosts remains problematic.

The Service Fee

In June 2019, Taobao Live announced that a service fee which accounts for 6% of selling price was to be charged, for using Taobao's livestream service to sell merchandise unregistered on the platform. The regulation allows Taobao to take a larger percentage of every host's earning from livestreams, whenever a product registered on any other platform is sold, which sorely harms the interests of the hosts and other livestream platforms such as Kwai. Before the regulation, to be specific, if a product registered on Kwai was sold on Taobao Live, the host and Kwai together got 18% of the selling price from the merchant as commission, while only 2% went to Alibaba who owns Taobao Live. Now thanks to the new rule, Alibaba gets a lot more and they get much less. On the one hand, for certain, this has further ensured Taobao Live's superiority in the industry, making the well-fortified ramparts even sturdier. On the other hand, the new remuneration means more abundant traffic and a more incentive mechanism that Alibaba can arrange to inspire ordinary hosts and upgrade their platforms, thus forming a positive feedback loop.

The Diversified Ecosystem to Come

Taobao Live's management once revealed in an internal seminar that in a few years, the company would invest ten billions RMB or more to reinforce the platform's livestream service, namely the "Ten Billion Sponsorship". Broadly, the whole plan will provide professional training and incentives for merchants, hosts, MCN agencies and other livestream practitioners, from which small and medium-sized businesses will benefit the most, getting more traffic and admissions to certain user interfaces. At the same time, Taobao Live will speed up the research and development of livestream technology to prepare for more innovations in the 5G era. The overall upgrade ought to be complete no longer than two years, as the management planned. It is a diversified, versatile livestream ecosystem Alibaba is expecting, in which all sorts of the company's online and offline resources such as e-commerce merchants, MCN organisations, livestream bases, target markets, newcome retailers and industry concentration areas are unexceptionally integrated. Alibaba believes it is the most efficient and effective way to energise the undervalued practitioners and the whole industry.

The Traffic Ceiling

In the past three years, the number of users and the market size of Taobao Live have been both on the rise, while acquiring more Internet traffic has proved to be the platform's top priority unchanged. The traffic profitability however, seeing from the slowdown of user growth and the increase in the relevant costs in recent years, has already reached the ceiling. Now, the platform is suffering from the ordeal of breaking the traffic limitation and acquiring more active users, despite the "Ten Billion Sponsorship" that has already been applied. This leaves the platform few workarounds but to alter the top priority from acquiring more traffic to looking for more reasonable and cost-effective means of traffic allocation, in order to increase the activeness of user engagement, which demands better livestream content and more varieties of merchandise.

1.2 Kwai

Overview

In 2019, the number of daily active users of Kwai reached 100 million, and the number of active merchants exceeded one million. More than 61% of the merchants had a monthly income of 100,000 RMB. As one of the top hosts of Kwai, Xin Ba's total GMV of livestreaming e-commerce reached 13.3 billion RMB in the same year. In May 2019, it was also on Kwai where Dong Mingzhu amazed the industry by selling 300 million yuan's goods in a 3-hour livestream. Currently, Kwai has over 600

MCN agencies installed and more than 6,000 hosts. Also, the platform's strong support for MCN institutions, coupled with its conservation of on-platform traffic, greatly promoted the development of its livestream service. Through the collaboration with multiple e-commerce platforms, Kwai did brilliantly in traffic monetisation. At present, Kwai, in addition to its own stores, has linked itself with numerous stores on Taobao, JD, Buy Together and other third-party e-commerce platforms. From initially an unaccompanied social networking platform whose main e-commerce function was to redirect users to e-commerce-oriented platforms such as Taobao, Kwai has evolved to a generalist that provides independent e-commerce service and equally cooperates with multiple forerunners, leveraging its Internet traffic to build transaction loops and cash flows round the clock.

Development Process

Since 2017, Kwai began to develop its livestreaming e-commerce strategy with two focuses. The first was to encourage user gratuity, which by then was appreciated by Kwai hosts as a main source of revenue. The second was to actuate hosts to post product links that lead audience to e-commerce-oriented platforms where they could shop, while audience were allowed to share the links on WeChat, Weibo and other platforms for wider dissemination. In June 2018, Kwai officially opened the first batch of its own stores that supported livestreaming e-commerce. Then, in October, the platform's marketing system was established, followed by Project Maitian released in December, which aimed at a new upgrade of traffic monetisation, with Kwai stores as the main beneficiaries. In June 2019, Kwai opened the door to Buy Together and started cooperating with WeChat and JD as well. A month later in July, Kwai launched Project Photosynthesis to support short video creators and livestream practitioners with more copious traffic supply. Then, in August, Kwai organised a shopping festival called "The Well Rated", looking to win consumer's trust with quality advantages. After that, Kwai arranged another shopping festival in November, which was named as "1106" by date, attempting to innovate from the operation side and build consumer awareness.

Characteristics

Large-Scale Traffic Monetisation

Since Kwai rarely performs manual intervention and traffic adjustment on content producing, a compatible relationship between the platform and the users depends on the latter's recognition. Once such relationship is established, it is rather steadfast. Originally being a social networking platform that lacked of commercial features, Kwai gives the hosts enough space to livestream unreservedly, hence the prosperity of the fan economy. Moreover, the platform's well-arranged conservation of on-platform traffic ensured that plenty of the waist and tail hosts have more chances to monetise, while the head hosts remain profitable. The sufficient traffic leads to a large-scale traffic monetisation, which has become Kwai's foremost competitive power. Even some tail hosts on Kwai, who have less than 100,000 fans, have proved they can make close to 1 million RMB with a single livestream.

Strong Support for Business Partners

Kwai's on-platform traffic conservation and Project Photosynthesis have been music to all the collaborators' ears. As early as Project Photosynthesis was launched, Kwai promised to join forces with over 2,000 business partners including MCN organisations, media companies, personal media and service providers, together to facilitate the traffic conservation, motivate content producers, promote traffic monetisation and upskill livestream influencers in this league, through IP sharing, multi-industry explorations and transregional cooperation. At the same time, Kwai provided 100,000 content producers with ten billion yuan's worth of traffic, helping them gain more exposure as well as raising a "creator's platform". Last but not least, the benefited producers were also granted access to the platform's public settlement, data centre and multi-account management system.

The Rich and Carefree Core Customers

Livestreaming e-commerce's strong monetisation ability owes much to the residents of minor cities. Currently, taking Taobao as an example, the sixth-tier cities in China have contributed most livestream audience, followed by the second- and the third-tier cities. And Kwai, whose penetration rate for audience who live in the cities below the third tier is as high as 58.9%, shows a similar user structure. The fact is not so surprising, since the COVID-19 epidemic has hammered China's economy rather hard, and people who live in smaller cities have less financial pressure than top-tier cities' inhabitants, but more needs due to the lack of consumption choices. And these "rich and carefree" consumers, on top of that, also have ample time for watching livestreams, which has naturally made them the leading platforms' core users. Such being the case, Kwai, as a veteran in the e-commerce industry and rather a social-networking platform than a commercial-oriented one, is both entertainingly attractive and a convenient option for online shopping, thus among the minority of Chinese enterprises that benefited profoundly from the economic disaster. With the core customers Kwai has harvested during the epidemic as the backbone of its business, it can either march to the cities of high tiers for a gold mining of new possibilities, or stay prudent for a more cost-effective expansion in the less developed areas, where it has planted the flag. And both ways seem to be feasible.

The Restricting Supply Chain

Awkward as it is for a leading livestream platform, Kwai by far is still struggling with the two-step procedure of monetisation, which means more often than not, it must direct users to other platforms such as Taobao and Buy Together so they can finalise purchases. For Kwai, it is as much a part of the cooperative agreements as a restriction that on the one hand has compensated for its deficiency in the supply of goods, which is not near integrated compared with Taobao's, and leads to some revenue losses on the other hand, like the 6% service fee charged by Taobao, for one, which is not negligible considering Kwai's strategy of large-scale monetisation. Facing the dilemma, Kwai chose to remain the two-step procedure as a mutual constraint and at the same time quicken the pace of building an independent e-commerce ecosystem. A resultant project was launched in 2020, namely "the project of accelerating Kwai's on-platform brand marketing" as a literal translation, showing that it is urgent for Kwai to build a more supportive and standardised supply chain to enrich the supply of goods and remove the restriction.

2 Strategy Principles of Main Livestream Platforms

2.1 Taobao Live: Cross-Level Incentive and Cloud Markets

At present, Taobao Live has over 400 million active users, with livestream scenes covering factories, farmlands, shopping malls, market stalls, fairs, retail outlets and outdoor sceneries in 73 countries around the world. It has become the starting point for many industries to embrace the new economy. Moreover, as results of the huge Internet traffic and more than 1000 MCN organisations installed, the total watch time of Livestreams on Taobao Live is 350,000 hours per day, 70, 000 times of the duration of a Spring Festival Gala, China's largest government-organised entertaining show. However, the highly unhealthy host structure remains a severe holdback for the platform's livestream service. According to the information released in March 2020 at Taobao's strategic management conference, the company's current strategy principle is to focus on supporting middle and low level hosts, while a total of 50 billion RMB is to invest in 100,000 hosts below the upper level, whose monthly income must be more than 10,000 RMB, but shall not be near as much as an upper level host's.

At the same time, Taobao Live has paid more attention to digital experiences. The plan is to open 100 "cloud market" across the country and bring 200,000 offline stores into the new economic ecosystem, building a digital highway that connects physical businesses and the online market. To achieve the goal, a multi-dimensional user interface on Taobao Live has been developed to offer comprehensive and integrated product instructions and marketing information, which are all highly graphical and designed intriguing to catch a prospective partner's eyes. In short, what Taobao expects is a versatile livestream ecosystem capable of incubating more occupations, attracting more resources and above all, escalating the expansion of its online territories.

2.2 Buy Together: Diversified Product Layout

Buy Together, namely Pinduoduo, one of the largest companies mainly profiting from organising group-buying in China, has also realised livestream may be the future backbone of their business. In January 2020, the company launched Duo Duo Live, starting to provide livestream service and develop three marketing models that fit the platform's changing features, which are named "Livestreaming", "Pinxiaoquan" (small-scale group-buying) and "Kuaituantuan" (offline group-buying). Products on Duo Duo Live are mostly agricultural products, jewelleries and apparels, which are also linked to the platform's mini programme on WeChat, for WeChat users to invite friends for a group-watching that may lead to a group-buying. Once a three-people group is formed, every member in the group gets a reward, such as a 50% discount coupon. Duo Duo Live positions itself as a marketing vessel for prospective partners that include not only professional platforms, but also average users, providing everyone with welfare as investments in future. For now, what the company most concerns for is assembling more users and making them stay for a higher conversation rate, with the platform's relatively enough supply of traffic.

In the meantime, Buy Together also intends to apply more specific regulations to bring more MCN organisations into partnership, making Duo Duo Live an all-round platform of diversification and integration. At the end of March 2020, Duo Duo Live got the first batch of MCNs in cooperation, who matched the following three conditions: 1. the business entity is qualified to issue special value-added tax invoices for cultural service fees, other brokerage agency service fees, livestream service fees and performance service fees. 2. It is experienced on other e-commerce platforms or has employees specialising in PGC (Professional Generated Content) or livestream hosting (the number of such employees is expected to be 10–20). 3. It agrees to join the partnership only as a MCN organisation.

2.3 JD: Forming a Hierarchy

Unlike Taobao, JD appears to care little build a versatile ecosystem for its livestream practitioners. Quite the opposite, the company prefers a hierarchical structure to the equality of opportunity. A series of JD's policies for incentive, such as those concerning double commissions, livestream quantity bonus, host ranking contests, supports for high-quality official accounts and "Project 2 + 2" formulated to be advantageous to the head hosts, mostly are aimed at but forming a hierarchy in which the best-performed gets the most. This makes "precise reinforcement" the keywords for JD's strategic principle. In addition, the company has implemented a full-year reward mechanism, which stipulates that the lowest percentage of commission submitted to the JD platform by a third party is 1%, which is, undoubtedly, a privilege that belongs to the most profit-making business entities. "The Horse Racing Mechanism" it is called, which was originally used as a governmental reward mechanism for the COVID-19 epidemic management, meaning the better the government officials control the disease, the better they get awarded. While applied on JD, it operates in the same way: different "horses" pay different commissions, depending on their "breeds".

Currently, JD intends to achieve three goals concerning livestreaming e-commerce, as in larger marketing size, better product quality and an elite-based ecosystem. To achieve the first, JD's intent is that its livestream content covers all the product categories and more than 60% of the merchants registered on the JD platform, as precise supports and comprehensive supports run concurrently. As for the second, JD means to improve the overall quality of livestream content, as well as to uplift host activeness and consumer acquisition ability. Lastly, JD appears to be confident that its well-awarded e-commerce experts, particularly those ones in millions, are energetic and resolved enough to lead the construction of a unique, elite-based ecosystem, and that the "elites" themselves are more than invigorative examples to invent the "ordinaries", only with a few aids of a more reasonable distribution of resources.

2.4 TikTok: Better Monetisation and On-Platform Store Upgrades

Sensing the change of wind direction, TikTok has been adjusting strategies same as its competitors. It was 2018 when the company entered the e-commerce industry, purposeful to monetise the considerable amount of traffic absorbed. At that time however, the platform's traffic distributing rules were based on content attributes, which was unfit for the conservation of on-platform traffic once the door was opened to the whole industry. Therefore, the platform's attraction to perspective business partners, such as MCN organisations, was far from strong. Resultantly in 2018, TikTok created a one-click shopping function for on-platform influencers who had over a million fans, which directed users to Taobao's homepage, to make purchases of products recommended by TikTok's influencers. This is namely the two-step shopping procedure TikTok and Kwai have endured till today.

Later in 2018, TikTok opened the first batch of its own online stores, the first step for e-commerce independence. Then, in April 2019,

TikTok's e-commerce business extended to JD and Xiaomi, accompanied by the launches of several relevant mini programmes that allowed users to finish purchases on the TikTok platform. So far, linking its own platform with third parties' and offering users with a closed-loop shopping experience seemed to be the best TikTok could make.

Since 2020, TikTok has begun to raise the entry barriers for livestreaming e-commerce. Measures include limiting the frequency of merchants posting commercial content, and how often such content can be posted depends on how many fans the account has. Also, a rule of account ranking has been applied to those who are authorised to post commercial content, including commercial livestreams. The platform states that the ranking is based on the levels of an account's content quality, influence, fan activities and commercial value. The higher the account's ranking, the more the owner's privileges. By the arguably one-sided standard, TikTok wishes to exclude low-quality content creators from the platform, as far as the revenue growth is unharmed, though doing so has inevitably made the platform much less diversified, as content rich in originality and artistic appealing now must make way for things that are commercially valuable.

In 2020, TikTok restarted the programme of self-established online stores that had been shelved for nearly a year and signed a contract with Luo Yonghao, the first-generation Internet influencer in China, whose commercial livestream debut gathered more than 48 million people to watch and achieved 110 million RMB in sales. Apparently, TikTok has chosen the path of a e-commerce-oriented platform over its initial social networking nature.

2.5 *Kwai: Self-Sufficiency and Cross-Platform Reciprocity*

Rather like TikTok, Kwai entered the livestream industry as a typical social-networking short video platform, whose inherent lack of e-commerce features told against it. Even today, many of TikTok's e-commerce-oriented add-ons, such as the one-click and direct shopping links, still cannot be found on Kwai. This results in that many hosts have to lead users to their own online stalls registered on third-party platforms. The insufficient on-platform resources drive Kwai hosts and users to a mutual need of outside trading communities, which have already been formed widely on WeChat Moments and Taobao. This is also a foregone conclusion since Kwai aims to monetise its huge traffic as practically as possible, but always concerns more for the on-platform traffic conservation.

Unwilling to be an e-commerce vessel for third parties, Kwai plans to maintain the partnership with other platforms and in the meantime endeavour to achieve self-sufficiency. Though Kwai's strategic layout is rather similar to TikTok's, it was conscious of the necessity of a self-built closed-loop system of e-commerce much earlier. Since 2018, it has already started establishing its own online stores, almost as soon as it reached an agreement of cross-platform reciprocity with Taobao, Youzan, Mokuai and other third parties. And "Project Photosynthesis", which was undisguisedly designed for promoting the platform's self-sufficiency, was announced soon after in 2019. Apart from offering additional traffic worthy of 10 billion RMB to 100,000 content creators in a year, the project also includes some elements of "precise reinforcement" like JD's, showing Kwai's determination to cultivate "elite" accounts competent to generate phenomenal content, as many as 3,000 that each owns at least one million fans. From the chosen 3,000 "elites", Kwai picked ten with most protuberant aptitudes for monetising, offering them customised supports, in the hope of making them exclusive IPs and spearheads of the platform's e-commerce ventures.

Furthermore, Kwai has proceeded to upgrade its livestream service in the areas of copyright protection, creating motivation and third-party operation. Upskilling on-platform MCN organisations was also put on the schedule. Meanwhile, the platform has started an exploration offline, seeking for regional cooperation with media groups, social networking accounts, personal media and MCNs throughout the country, diversifying its offline layout. For example, it has been working with some gourmet accounts to convert the online popularities to the relevant physical stores' prosperities, or in other words, to convert the traffic absorbed to offline revenues. Since the physical stores are related to Kwai in different ways, it is one of the many forms of closed-loop self-sufficiency. And other than that, it connects the physical and digital layers of a certain market with vertical customers and enhances cross-industry cooperation.

2.6 Red: The B2K2C Closed-Loop and Brand-Based Livestreams

Quite different from e-commerce platforms that are attentive to livestream content, such as Weibo and Bilibili, Red has developed a monetisation method that combines e-commerce and advertising. Since 2013, Red has seen young women as its core users and put much effort into generating huge amount of female-oriented content, mainly concerning beauty, fashion and travel. Consequently, this has formed the special KOC (Key Opinion Customer)-based ecosystem of Red, making it essential that Red's content generators emotionally connect with users.

Usually, a business entity is forced to choose between marketing and livestreaming e-commerce as its sole occupation on Red. Whichever is chosen, a satisfying outcome lies in Red's brand-promoting advantage. One of the reasons why Red has brought plenty of influential brands into partnership is that the platform has created a B2K2C closed loop, in which brands and KOCs form a symbiotic relationship—brands need KOCs to target more vertical customers, and KOCs need brands to gain popularity and acquire more vertical fans, in their areas of expertise that intertwines with brand values. This may open a new path of sustainable development for livestreaming e-commerce, if more commercial livestreams and brand-based livestreams that are highly vertical with each other show greater potential of monetisation than those that are not. This is very likely happening, judging by the data that shows Red's overall conversion rate in livestreaming e-commerce is higher than its competitors, for now at least.[1]

Red seems to be aware of this. In 2020, the company released a brand support plan, promising.

zero admission charge, commission discount and traffic support, to reduce hosts' livestreaming costs and uplift over 10,000 newly joined brands, while 200 top-ranking account owners and 100 new product categories were also benefited.

3 Case Analysis

3.1 Qianxun Group: The MCN Agency Behind Viya

MCN agencies are important platforms that provide intermediary services, connecting brand resources with livestream hosts. In the field of livestreaming e-commerce, supply chain resources are the core resources

[1] Jiang Xiaoting. "Second half of the Livestream Game: Red Made a Breakthrough", posted by WeChat Official Account "Zimubang", released on July 26, 2020. https://mp.weixin.qq.com/s/QLvCKCTcKjMwQOF3ckY0nw.

of MCN agencies. A competitive MCN agency needs to have an edge in sourcing and selecting reliable products. Usually, platforms such as TikTok and Kwai will build their own livestream bases to integrate resources and offer suitable products to MCN agencies which cooperate with them. While the company Qianxun Group known for China's top livestream host Viya, and the company Mei ONE famous for Li Jiaqi have broken through the developing boundaries of normal MCN organisations. With professional talent management and supply chain management as their key competitive advantages, they are able to coordinate resources to the maximum so as to empower livestream hosts and achieve traffic monetisation.

When the enterprise called Qianxun Group was first established at the end of 2016, with only four employees, its purpose was to form a competent management team for Viya. In late 2018, inspired by the mainstream trend of "content is king", Qianxun set a new goal to become the top MCN organisation in the livestream industry. Now that wish has come true, Qianxun intends to provide operational support to other MCN organisations. Apart from influencers, Qianxun has also signed contracts with a group of Chinese celebrities including well-known hosts and actors in order to realise the subdivision of livestream resources and differentiated marketing.

It is worth mentioning that Qianxun has reached a strategic cooperation with Xi'an United Nation Quality Detection Technologies Joint Stock Company Limited, the largest comprehensive third-party testing institute in northwest China. They jointly establish a quality control centre and a comprehensive product quality evaluation system. In that way, Qianxun improves the product selection mechanism of livestream rooms. At the same time, Qianxun has launched the "Super Supply Chain Base", which will be open to other MCN organisations in future, realising the full product category coverage. This not only simplifies the investment-attracting procedures for livestream hosts, but also helps businesses find more suitable host candidates at a lower cost.

3.2 Zhihu: Q&A Jumping in Livestreaming E-Commerce

Zhihu, Quora's Chinese equivalent as well as China's biggest online community, is home to 315 million questions and answers contributed by 43 million content creators, the number of whose monthly active users reached 76 million in the fourth quarter of 2020. In July 2020, Zhihu held its first commercial livestream to promote the platform's marketing resources. During the livestream, famed content creators on Zhihu acted as hosts and showed the audience innovative commercialisation solutions as well as successful marketing cases of the platform, effectively communicating with brands while gaining both attention and recognition for the platform. The creative event proves that commercial livestreams can not only help with selling physical products, but also provide monetisation opportunities for intangible content resources, which is of great significance for the online paid knowledge industry.

3.3 *Chinese TV Stations' Multi-Path Exploration of Livestreaming E-Commerce*

Livestreaming e-commerce in recent years has provided a viable transformation and upgrading path for traditional television stations, which have suffered a significant decline in revenue from the impact of new media. That is, with the technical support of Internet platforms, TV stations can make the best of their own influence and the popularity of eminent anchors to build an MCN mechanism, transforming the audience into consumers and obtaining advertising revenue from brands through commercial livestreams.

The pandemic in 2020 has directly accelerated the process of building MCN mechanisms for a number of Chinese TV stations including CCTV (China Central Television), China's predominant state-owned TV station. CCTV has made several achievements in the field of livestreaming e-commerce. A livestream concentrating on selling household appliances and digital products was hosted by four famous CCTV anchors on the evening of May 1, 2020. In the end, the livestream had a cumulative total of 24 million viewers from the CCTV News application, TikTok, JD, Buy Together and other e-commerce platforms, with the sales reaching a staggering 520 million RMB.

Together with Tencent, CNRmall also held several large-scale livestreaming e-commerce activities in 2020 to help farmers in remote and impoverished areas increase the sales of agricultural and sideline products. A number of Chinese county governors were invited to the livestream room to endorse local products, thus attracting more traffic for the livestream as well as contributing to considerable sales.

Besides national TV stations, provincial TV stations are also actively making innovative attempts in livestreaming e-commerce. Hunan TV, a provincial satellite TV station based in Hunan Province, owns currently China's second-most-watched channel, second only to CCTV-1. During 2020, Hunan TV invited Viya to participate in its ace reality show, where Viya organised a livestream to sell unsalable fruits due to the pandemic. Eventually, the total sales reached more than 5.2 million yuan, benefiting 1750 farmers from 195 villages of Yunnan Province. Similar practice was carried out by Dragon TV in Shanghai. Under Viya's guidance, the livestream in the reality show prompted over 200 thousand items to be sold out in 40 minutes. Meanwhile, Shandong TV launched a programme called "Hometown Goodies", inviting county governors from Shandong Province to introduce regional specialties, and users could watch commercial livestreams on Taobao, TikTok and Kwai, purchasing recommended products.

Some municipal TV stations also deserve recognition for their exploration. Jinan is the capital city of China's Shandong Province. Jinan TV has taken the lead in cooperating with professional MCN agencies to build its own MCN brand and carry out commercial livestreams. By employing new marketing methods, Jinan TV hopes to stimulate consumption and provide new momentum for regional economic development after the pandemic.

CHAPTER 5

Risks and Future of Livestreaming E-Commerce in China

Abstract This chapter analyses potential risks of livestreaming e-commerce and proposes possible solutions to the existing problems. The industrial risks not only relate to host obligations and legal relationships between MCN agencies and hosts, but can be associated with product selection as well. The construction of a healthy industrial ecology requires the joint efforts of livestreamers, MCN agencies, livestreaming platforms and government regulators. This chapter also predicts the future of livestreaming e-commerce in the post-pandemic era, putting forward five main trends: supply chain upgrading accelerates industry standardisation; livestreaming e-commerce develops in coordination with more industries; professional backgrounds of livestreamers become more diversified; the long tail effect boosts the expansion of livestreaming e-commerce market; digital operation management helps to accurately meet consumers' needs.

Keywords Risk aversion · Legal relationship · Supply chain optimization · Long tail effect

R. Si, *China Livestreaming E-commerce Industry Insights*, https://doi.org/10.1007/978-981-16-5344-5_5

1 Industrial Risk Assessment and Possible Solutions

In the 1960s, French philosopher Guy Debord put forward the concept of "society of the spectacle", and in 2002, American cultural critic Douglas Kellner developed Debord's theory, proposing the concept of media spectacle to refer to technologically mediated events in contemporary socio-cultural context. Livestreaming e-commerce has created a media spectacle with Chinese characteristics over the past few years.[1] Wu Xiaobo, a well-known Chinese financial writer, regards livestreaming e-commerce as the most exciting business experiment of 2020. According to statistics, by the end of 2020, the sales of livestreaming e-commerce in China will exceed one trillion yuan and will account for one-fifth of the total sales of China's e-commerce by 2021.

Despite the extreme popularity of livestreaming e-commerce, there exist some potential industrial risks that need to be avoided, including risks from hosts' personal branding or the legal relationship between hosts and MCN agencies as well as risks from the selection of products. This section will analyse these risks and suggest possible solutions to them.

1.1 Risk Analysis of Hosts

The industrial risks of livestreaming e-commerce are mainly related to hosts. As the undoubted protagonist of the livestream room, hosts take responsibility for controlling the livestream's pace and interacting with viewers. They are supposed to develop personalised marketing strategies based on the characteristics of different products, thus building their personal brands. As viewers can realise active virtual participation in the livestream by making real-time comments, opinions expressed by hosts naturally provide topics for them to discuss, which may lead to potential public controversy. Viewers who have previously placed orders may share their consumption experiences through comments. Their comments, if positive, will promote the word-of-mouth marketing of specific products,

[1] Huang Zhongjun, Jiang Zhihan, *A New Vanity Fair in the Consumer Era: A Study of Celebrities' Participation in Livestreaming E-Commerce*, Journal of School of Chinese Language and Culture of Nanjing Normal University, 2020 (04).

while negative comments could directly harm traffic monetisation of the livestreaming, even damaging hosts' public images.[2]

Therefore, livestream hosts' self-discipline should be paid more attention to. Currently, the government's regulatory departments and livestream platforms have both introduced strict regulations for hosts. For instance, hosts are required to provide valid personal information such as their ID numbers when registering on any e-commerce platform. The venues and content of livestream should also comply with relevant laws and platform rules.

Considering livestreaming e-commerce is a special kind of online marketing activity, the judgement of legal liability associated with it needs to be made on a case-by-case basis. When hosts sell their own products, they are the seller and should obey the Contract Law. While if they just promote products for brands, they are bound by the relevant provisions in the Advertising Law.

The obligations of hosts contain prompting consumers with information concerning their life and safety, no private cross-platform transactions, no data fraud, etc. It is also not allowed to defraud commission by means of fake orders or malicious return deliveries. These obligations are from laws such as the Advertising Law, the Law on the Protection of Consumer Rights and Interests and the Law against Unfair Competition. If a host violates legal obligations to a certain extent, it's very likely that he or she will be punished according to the Criminal Law.

1.2 Legal Relationships Between MCN Agencies and Livestream Hosts

In China, e-commerce giants and some social media provide platforms for livestream hosts to promote products. It is necessary for platforms to construct a sound regulation system and implement differentiated management based on specific circumstances of businesses, better protecting consumer interests and intellectual property rights. On the one hand, livestream hosts set up personal accounts on certain platform and accumulate their raw audience with the platform's traffic recommendation. On the other hand, hosts also need support from professional MCN

[2] Shen Yang, Yan Jiaqi, *How to Prevent Risks of Livestreaming E-Commerce,* New Media, 2021 (01).

agencies to achieve constant output of high-quality content and traffic monetisation.

MCN agencies provide services for livestream hosts. According to the Code of Conduct for Livestream Marketing issued by the China Advertising Association, the functions of these service organisations are mainly divided into cultivating livestream hosts and offering support for commercial livestreams. MCN agencies shall be responsible for livestream activities of their contracted hosts.[3] Therefore, the legal relationship between hosts and MCN agencies is closely related to the interests of both parties and their long-term cooperation. It has become a common risk faced by China's livestreaming e-commerce industry that MCN agencies deliberately damage hosts' interests.

The legal relationship between livestream hosts and MCN agencies is usually determined by agreement. In addition to the labour agreement requiring hosts to provide labour services for the MCN agency upon request, agreements signed often include the brokerage agreement, which stipulates that the MCN agency and the host are partners. As the exclusive broker of the host, the MCN agency has the right to arrange all business activities. The host must obey the business arrangements and other requirements. Both parties shall share the livestream revenues according to the agreed proportion, and the agency isn't obliged to make contributions to the statutory social insurance and housing schemes for the host.[4]

There are mainly three types of relationships between MCN agencies and hosts. The first type is labour relationship, where hosts are subject to the agency's management. The second type is service relationship, where both parties are equal in legal status, and the host can freely negotiate with the agency on their rights and obligations. The third type is business cooperation relationship: the host independently takes charge of continuous content creation and output, and the MCN agency just provides support services including brand resource recommendation, account operation, fan management, etc. From a legal perspective,

[3] Xiang Jiang, *China Advertising Association Releases "Regulation on Product Selection in Livestreaming E-Commerce", Top MCN Agencies Make Self-Discipline Commitments*, China Consumer Journal, https://mp.weixin.qq.com/s/Lzh1BSbch9BZkqIiBcda7g.

[4] Gao Yaping, Zhou Meng, Ji Qian, *Decoding Legal Relationships Between Livestream Hosts and MCN Agencies*, DeHeng Law Offices, April 22, 2020, https://mp.weixin.qq.com/s/hB56RFwVwnnH0jxG4gGylQ.

Table 1 This chart mainly illustrates the type of legal relationship between host and MCN agencies, tax item, tax rate, taxpayer, withholding agent

Legal relationship	*Tax item*	*Tax rate (%)*	*Taxpayer*	*Withholding agent*
Labour relationship	Income derived from wages and salaries	3–45	Livestream host	MCN agency
Service relationship	Income derived from remuneration for personal services	3–45	Livestream host	MCN agency
Cooperation relationship	Income from business operation	3–45	Livestream host	–

different relationships also determine the tax obligations of the host and the MCN agency differently (Table 1).

In recent years, the conflict between hosts and MCN agencies has aroused more attention, prompting the industry to consider how to deal with such legal risks. For hosts, when choosing an MCN agency to sign up with, they should carefully review the agency's qualifications to avoid potential disputes. Also, when discussing details of the agreement with the agency, they should ensure that the rights and obligations of both parties are clearly defined. For MCN agencies, they are supposed to take both their own resources and hosts' influence into account when drawing up contracts, communicating with hosts effectively about ownership of intellectual property rights and non-compete clause. Meanwhile, they should set up a stable fee payment and data retention mechanism throughout the partnership.

The focus of agreements between MCN agencies and different types of hosts varies. For hosts with special professional backgrounds who mainly create high-quality content, they should concentrate on clauses concerning the lasting time and content of livestreaming. While for hosts who mainly offer promotion services, the number of advertisements and advertising frequency need to be paid more attention to. For hosts directly selling products, they should focus on the ownership and use of platform accounts.[5]

Based on the above analysis, the construction of a transparent and healthy industrial ecology for livestreaming e-commerce requires the joint efforts of hosts, MCN agencies, livestream platforms and government regulators. To promote the positive development of the whole industry in the long run, both promoting policies and standardised guidance are necessary.

1.3 Risk Analysis of Product Selection

The uncontrollable risks of livestreaming e-commerce sometimes come from product selection. Currently, problems such as exaggerated promotion and lack of after-sales guarantee still occur. Effective product selection management can significantly reduce potential risks.

For commercial considerations, livestream hosts need to strictly control the quality of their products to earn customers' trust. There are three aspects they should pay attention to when selecting products for sale. First, to enhance the credibility of their sales pitch, hosts should consider whether the type of products they promote is in accordance with their public images. Second, priority needs to be given to products of which customers don't need much time to make purchase decisions. These kind of products are often necessities with low prices, such as food and household essentials. Third, hosts should choose personalised products that are easy to display in the livestream room, such as cosmetics and accessories.[6] For the products promoted in the livestreaming, apart from the price and product quality reflected in the form of testing reports, selection indicators also include the manufacturer's supply capacity, delivery speed and after-sales service. According to the top host Li Jiaqi, there are professional staff specifically in charge of product selection in his team. He not only sells products, but also empowers brands.

[5] Gao Yaping, Zhou Meng, Ji Qian, How to Build a Perfect Relationship Between Livestream Hosts and MCN Agencies, DeHeng Law Offices, Mar 18, 2020, https://mp.weixin.qq.com/s/HUblDpVJgaqoJ6aJgk3M4Q.

[6] Shen Yang, Yan Jiaqi, *How to Prevent Risks of Livestreaming E-Commerce*, New Media, 2021 (01).

2 Future of Livestreaming E-Commerce in the Post-Pandemic Era

2.1 Supply Chain Upgrade Accelerating Industry Standardisation

Since the launch of Taobao Live in 2016, livestreaming e-commerce has been developing prosperously. The empowerment of new technologies such as AR, VR and artificial intelligence will promote the shaping of its closed-loop ecological chain. With the help of big data and cloud computing, the supply chain will be completely upgraded, all taches of which including design and production, quality evaluation, omni-channel marketing and package delivery will synchronise in development with livestreaming e-commerce.

Nowadays, users' browsing data is all recorded and collected, thus forming a huge database. As a result, with the assistance of recommendation algorithms, livestreaming e-commerce can not only accurately meet the current needs of users, but also find their potential needs, providing relevant services in advance. The customer-to-manufacturer business model, also known as C2M, connects manufacturers and consumers directly, enabling factories to produce on demand and control costs. Moreover, the combination of the C2M model and short videos helps to promote more targeted supply of reserves and more efficient sales.[7]

2.2 Development in Coordination with More Industries

The COVID-19 pandemic in 2020 has brought livestreaming e-commerce unprecedented popularity, and in the post-epidemic era, livestreaming e-commerce will become a new economic form. Unlike live fashion shows and gaming livestreams, commercial livestreams provide an immersive experience for viewers through real-time social interaction, creative marketing strategies and creating a sense of urgency. In the age of intelligent media, livestreaming e-commerce will develop in coordination with more industries. In addition to the economic value of traffic monetisation, it will also better realise social value in areas like poverty alleviation and government communication, strengthening its public attribute.

[7] Chen Hedan, You Keke, Zhang Jinwen, *A New Study on Life, Communication and Consumption Value of Short Videos,* Journal of Communication and Society, 2021 (01).

2.3 Professional Backgrounds of Diversified Hosts

In future, as the number of hosts keeps increasing on a large scale, professional backgrounds of livestream hosts will become more diverse. Hosts will not be limited to influencers contracted by MCN organisations. Anchors from mainstream media, government officials, corporate CEOs, craftsmen, self-employed businessmen and even ordinary Chinese youths from small towns or vocaloid stars loved by Generation Z can become hosts.

Within a certain business cycle, if opinion leaders such as well-known anchors serve as livestream hosts, their credibility can both bring the livestreaming traffic and guarantee a high repeat purchase rate. It should be noted that at present some people who lack rational judgement participate in livestreaming e-commerce blindly, which can easily bring about industrial risks and should raise relevant departments' alert. It is necessary to judge the suitability of personal abilities to industry requirements before choosing livestreaming as a career.

2.4 Long Tail Effect Boosting the Market

American writer Chris Anderson introduced the concept of the "long tail" in 2004 to describe the business model of websites such as Amazon and Netflix. Long tail theory demonstrates the huge economic potential of niche markets[8] and can also be applied to livestreaming e-commerce.

With the support of big data and decentralised recommendation algorithms, niche products such as excavators and jade also have their own vertical audience in livestreaming e-commerce as popular categories like beauty products do, which provides the possibility of category verticalisation for livestreaming products and helps to further expand the market. In addition, some special agricultural products and handicrafts catering to consumers' curiosity as well as products with a high consumption threshold can also maximise the long tail effect if promoted in a proper way.

[8] (US) Chris Anderson, *The Long Tail: Why the Future of Business Is Selling Less of More*, CITIC Press Group, January 2021.

2.5 Digital Operation Management for Consumers' Needs

As another important participating body in livestreaming e-commerce apart from hosts, brands hope that commercial livestreams will both increase brand awareness and generate considerable sales. In accordance with the development of media technology, the digital operation practice of brands is also deepening. Brands can not only realise the intelligent service management, able to design attractive marketing strategies based on specific consumption scenarios such as new product launches and festival promotion, but also form accurate judgements on users' spending power, consumption willingness and consumption satisfaction according to the collected user data, adjusting marketing strategies in time.

Conclusion

After a large-scale expansion in 2020, China's livestreaming e-commerce industry has gained unprecedented attention while some problems have also prompted widespread social reflection, pushing for the formation of a more sound regulatory system. Considering effective epidemic prevention and control of China, successful resumption of work and production, and stable recovery of China's economy, people tend to doubt whether the strong demand for livestreaming e-commerce will continue to grow normally in the post-pandemic era.

Actually we are not only concerned with the development of communication technology or new media forms such as livestreaming, but also with grassroots innovation and cultural expressions. While livestreaming e-commerce brings ordinary individuals carnival experiences, as a democratic and free field, the livestreaming room also attracts countless viewers to immerse themselves in it.

This work discusses the developing trends of livestreaming e-commerce industry. Shaped by economic, policy, social and other forces, China's livestreaming e-commerce is not an accidental outcome, but an inevitable result of media development. As a more dynamic industry, it will have the potential to become a pillar industry of the national economy in future.

R. Si, *China Livestreaming E-commerce Industry Insights*,
https://doi.org/10.1007/978-981-16-5344-5

The manufacturer's authorised representative in the EU is Springer Nature Customer Service Centre GmbH, Europaplatz 3, 69115 Heidelberg, Germany. If you have any concerns regarding our products, please contact ProductSafety@springernature.com

Printed and bound by CPI Group (UK) Ltd, Croydon, CR0 4YY
30/09/2026
02225514-0003